PANAMA
AND THE
UNITED STATES

PANAMA

AND THE

UNITED STATES

~ ~ ~

DIVIDED
BY THE CANAL

~ ~ ~

Edmund Lindop

TWENTY-FIRST CENTURY BOOKS
A Division of Henry Holt and Company
New York

Twenty-First Century Books
A Division of Henry Holt and Company, Inc.
115 West 18th Street
New York, NY 10011

Henry Holt® and colophon are trademarks of
Henry Holt and Company, Inc.
Publishers since 1866

Published in Canada by Fitzhenry & Whiteside Ltd.
195 Allstate Parkway, Markham, Ontario L3R 4T8

Library of Congress Cataloging-in-Publication Data
Lindop, Edmund.
Panama and the United States: divided by the Canal / Edmund Lindop.
p. cm.
Includes bibliographical references and index.
Summary: Discusses foreign policy issues between the
United States and Panama, specifically regarding the Canal.
1. United States—Foreign relations—Panama—Juvenile literature.
2. Panama—Foreign relations—United States—Juvenile literature.
3. Panama Canal (Panama)—Juvenile literature. [1. United States—
Foreign relations—Panama. 2. Panama—Foreign relations—
United States. 3. Panama Canal (Panama)] I. Title.
E183.8.P2L47   1997   96-40948
327.7307287—dc21   CIP
                                               AC

ISBN 0-8050-4768-9
First Edition—1997

DESIGNED BY KELLY SOONG

Printed in Mexico
All first editions are printed on acid-free paper. ∞
1 3 5 7 9 10 8 6 4 2

Photo credits
p. 16: WorldSat International/Science Source/Photo Researchers, Inc.; p. 28 (all
three): Culver Pictures, Inc.; p. 44: Stephen Ferry/Gamma Liaison; p. 64: Owen
D.B./Black Star; p. 76: P.F. Bentley/Black Star; p. 90: R. Richard/Gamma Liaison; p. 100: Peter Jordan/Gamma Liaison.

~ ~ ~

For Joe Jares,
former student, outstanding writer,
sports expert, and cherished friend

CONTENTS

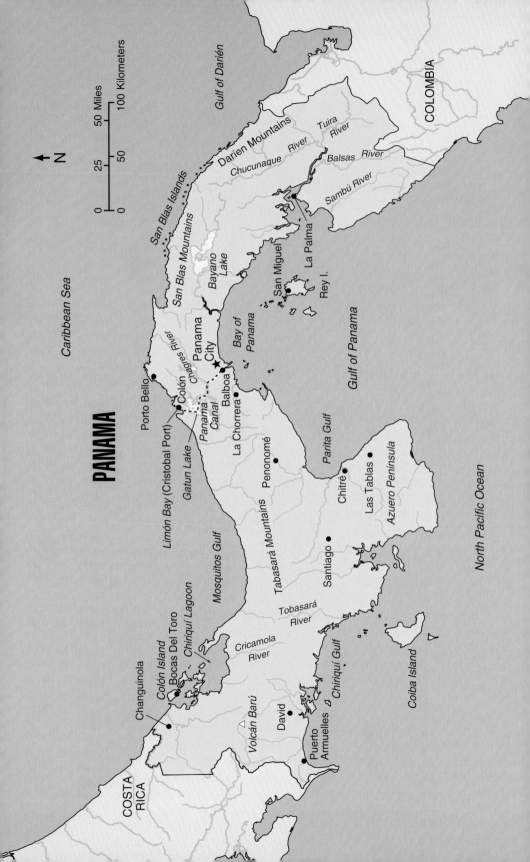

1

~ ~ ~

THE LAND AND
PEOPLE OF PANAMA

"Panama is a country whose history has been shaped by its geography," said Vice President Ricardo Arias Calderón in May 1991.[1] This is because Panama has a strategic location—it provides the shortest route between the Atlantic and Pacific Oceans. Since the 1500s the idea of crossing Panama has attracted widespread attention. First it was crossed on foot, later by railroad, and finally by a canal. In the twentieth century people in the United States have had a special interest in Panama because the canal that finally joined the two oceans was constructed, financed, operated, and protected by the U.S. government.

THE LAND

An isthmus connecting the continents of North America and South America, Panama is shaped like the letter S lying on its back. The country stretches in an east-west direction. The Pacific Ocean lies to its south; the Atlantic Ocean lies to its north. From some parts of Panama it is possible to watch the sun rise above the Pacific Ocean and set below the Caribbean Sea, which is an arm of the Atlantic Ocean.

Central America is the southernmost part of the North American continent, and Panama is the southernmost country in Central America. To the northwest is Costa Rica, Panama's nearest Central American neighbor. To the southeast is the South American country of Colombia, which owned Panama until the early 1900s.

Panama is a small country that covers an area of not quite 30,000 square miles. It is a little smaller than the state of South Carolina. The shortest distance across the isthmus is about 30 miles, and the longest distance is about 130 miles.

Along Panama's long, curving coastlines lie many scattered islands. The most important are the San Blas group in the Caribbean Sea and the Pearl Islands in the Pacific Ocean.

Near the middle of the country the Panama Canal bisects the isthmus, dividing it into western and eastern regions. The western region has the most productive farmland. The eastern region, except for the area near the canal, is sparsely populated and has less fertile farmland. Lowlands lie along both the Pacific and Caribbean coasts, and they provide most of the nation's crops.

A chain of mountains extends through the central part of Panama. The highest mountains are at either end of the country. The tallest peak, Volcán Barú, rises 11,400 feet near the Costa Rican border. The mountains decrease to their lowest altitudes at the nation's midpoint, and near the Panama Canal they reach a height of only a few hundred feet.

Panama is a tropical land with a climate that is usually

hot and humid, except in the mountain elevations. In the lowlands the temperature seldom drops below 80° F. Rainfall is heaviest on the Caribbean side, where it ranges annually from about 128 inches to 155 inches. Along the Pacific side the rainfall averages a little less than 70 inches, and there often is a winter season of a few months with almost no rain.

Tropical rain forests and thick jungle growth cover many of the areas that have heavy rainfall. Near the border with Colombia is one of the world's densest jungles, known as the Darién Gap. Largely because of the Darién Gap's rugged terrain, a section of the Pan-American Highway, which links North America to South America, has not been completed. Motorists traveling southward along this highway have to ship their cars by ferry from ports in Panama to Colombia or Venezuela.

Because of its tropical climate and large areas of thinly settled land, Panama has many animals that people in the United States seldom see except in zoos. These include jaguars, pumas, wild boars, armadillos, anteaters, many species of monkeys, and three-toed sloths hanging head down and moving slowly among the treetops.

TRADE

Bananas, sugar, and coffee are among Panama's leading agricultural exports. For domestic consumption, grains, vegetables, and a variety of fruits are raised. Both corn and rice are grown, but in Panama—unlike in other Central American countries and Mexico—rice is generally more common in the diet than corn.

The word *Panama* means "the land where fish are plentiful" in an Indian dialect.[2] Fish products constitute an important part of the nation's economy. Nearly a fifth of Panama's foreign income is earned from the sale of shrimp and fish meal, a product that is processed by grinding a small fish called the anchovetta.

Oil refining has become one of Panama's chief industries. Petroleum imported from Venezuela, Mexico, and Ecuador is processed in refineries that supply fuel mainly for ships and aircraft. Refined sugar, beverages, cement, and such consumer goods as clothing and shoes are other industrial products.

The United States is Panama's number-one trading partner. About half of Panama's exports go to the United States, and about one-third of its imports are U.S. products.

THE PEOPLE

There are about 2.5 million Panamanians. The original inhabitants of Panama were Indians, who lived there when the Spaniards colonized the isthmus in the 1500s. Some historians believe that when the Spaniards arrived there may have been one-half million Indians in Panama; other experts claim that one major tribe alone—the Cuna—accounted for 750,000 people.[3] Large numbers of Indians became victims of diseases unintentionally introduced by the Spaniards, and others died from the harsh treatment imposed on them by their conquerors. Today Indians make up only about 6 percent of the country's population. Many of these people inhabit the San Blas Islands and live much as their ancestors did centuries ago.

Black descendants of African slaves were brought from the islands of the West Indies to Panama in the 1850s to build the first railroad across the isthmus. Later, large numbers of West Indian blacks came to Panama to provide much of the hard physical labor needed to construct the canal.

Through the years, both Indians and blacks often married white people. Panamanians with a mixed Indian and white heritage are mestizos, and those with a mixed black and white heritage are mulattoes. Today more than 70 percent of Panama's people are mestizos or mulattoes. Whites and blacks each make up a little more than 10 percent of Panama's population. Smaller numbers of Asians also live in this racially diverse nation.

The country's official language is Spanish, but many Panamanians also speak and read English, and some newspapers are printed in both languages. The people of Panama are proud of the progress they have made in education. In 1911 only about a fourth of the population could read and write. Today the literacy rate is 88 percent.

Panama has freedom of religion. About 85 percent of its people are Roman Catholics; others are Protestants, Buddhists, Muslims, and Jews.

Slightly more than half of all Panamanians live in urban areas. Many of these people reside in two cities and their suburbs at the ends of the canal—Panama City, the nation's capital, on the Pacific side, and Colón on the Caribbean side. Panama City, with a population of more than 400,000, is the country's largest metropolitan area. Another major city, San Miguelito, is a short distance northeast of Panama City.

Chiefly because the country has large areas of mountains, tropical forests, and jungles, only about one-fourth of Panama's land can be cultivated. Some of the farmers work on banana and sugarcane plantations. A larger number of rural inhabitants barely eke out a living on small farms and mainly raise food crops for their families.

As in most Latin American nations, there are great extremes of wealth in Panama. A small number of families are rich, own elegant homes and expensive cars, and employ personal servants. Some of them own large tracts of land. Others are wealthy merchants, bankers, and professional people, such as doctors and lawyers. The middle class consists chiefly of shopkeepers, office workers, police and military personnel, and people whose jobs are related to the operation of the Panama Canal and the trade it promotes. The large class of poor people includes farmers with small plots of land, workers who toil on the plantations, many city laborers, and sidewalk vendors who sell their wares to tourists.

GOVERNMENT

The famous canal that joins together two huge oceans has been called the heart of modern Panama. The country's political affairs in the twentieth century have been dominated by fierce arguments with the United States over the control of the Canal Zone and the operation of the canal. Also, chiefly because of the canal, the presence of the United States in Panama has been of enormous economic importance to this small Central American nation.

For many years the government of Panama was frequently overthrown and run by rapidly changing leaders. After achieving independence in 1903, Panama had many presidents or dictators in the next sixty-five years. Between 1968 and 1989 the presidents of Panama were puppets controlled by military leaders. Since 1990 civilian presidents have headed the Panamanian government.

Unlike most other countries, Panama has two vice presidents. They divide the duties of the office. Five-year terms are served by the president and vice presidents; at the end of their terms they cannot run for reelection. The cabinet consists of twelve members appointed by the president.

The legislative, or lawmaking, power of the Panamanian government is vested in the National Assembly. Different from the United States Congress that consists of the Senate and the House of Representatives, the National Assembly is a one-house legislature. The lawmakers are also elected for five-year terms, and they can be reelected.

*This satellite image shows the North American continent.
The tiny Isthmus of Panama runs east-west and connects the
North American continent to the South American continent.*

2

~ ~ ~

CROSSROADS
OF THE WORLD

In 1502 Christopher Columbus stopped briefly on the coast of Panama during his fourth and final visit to the New World. Columbus, however, was not the first European to reach Panama. Spanish explorer Rodrigo de Bastidas commanded an expedition that landed on the isthmus during the spring of 1501. Seeking gold, Bastidas and his men searched a hundred-mile area before returning empty-handed to their ships.

FINDING AN OCEAN

Vasco Nuñez de Balboa was a member of Bastidas's crew. Following the ill-fated expedition to the Panama coast, Balboa became a farmer on Hispaniola, an island in the West Indies. He stayed on the island nine years. During this time he acquired many debts and had no idea how he was ever going to pay them off.

Then, in 1510, Balboa learned that an expedition was leaving Hispaniola, and its two ships would be sailing along the coast he had already explored. The expedition's leader, Martin Enciso, ordered several barrels of food from Balboa's farm. This gave Balboa a daring idea. He delivered the food and took aboard ship one empty barrel with a few holes in its sides. Then he crept into this barrel and pulled the lid down over his head.

After the ship set out on its voyage, the stowaway emerged from his hiding place. Enciso was furious when he discovered Balboa and threatened to throw him overboard, which was one of the customary punishments for stowaways. Balboa promised he would work hard for his passage and convinced Enciso that he could be helpful because he had already visited the land to which they were headed.

The ship sailed into the Gulf of Darién, and the Spaniards started a small settlement on the Caribbean side of Panama. The men did not like Enciso, who was cruel and told them they could not keep for themselves any of the gold they might find. So the Spaniards refused to continue taking orders from Enciso and turned to Balboa as their new leader.

For nearly three years Balboa and his followers hunted in vain for deposits of gold. Once they came upon a small Indian village, where the chief gave the Spaniards some gold ornaments. The chief's son explained to Balboa's interpreter, "I know where you can find all the gold that you want." Pointing toward the west, he continued, "Beyond those high mountains is a large sea. And beyond the sea is a land where there is plenty of gold."[1]

Balboa began his journey to find the large sea with 190 Spaniards and about 1,000 Indians to carry supplies and act as guides. For three weeks they tramped through mosquito-filled swamps and jungles crowded with tall trees, vines, and bushes that were so thick they blotted out the sunlight. Then they climbed steep, treacherous mountainsides. From the crest of one mountain, on September 25, 1513, Balboa sighted the huge sea that the Indian had described. Since it lay to his south, he called it the South Sea, but later it was renamed the Pacific Ocean.

Balboa, however, was not permitted to explore the vast ocean he had found. After his discovery he sent an envoy to the king of Spain, seeking royal permission to continue his expedition and be named governor of all the land that he claimed for Spain. But the king had already appointed a new governor of Panama, who falsely charged Balboa with treason and had him executed in January 1519.

PANAMA CITY

Panama City was founded on the Pacific shore in 1519. The chief port on the Caribbean Sea was Porto Bello (originally called Nombre de Dios). Indians constructed the first trail that crossed the isthmus and linked Panama City to Porto Bello. Extending about forty miles, it was a narrow stone path, barely wide enough for the mules that carried goods strapped to their backs. The trail was called El Camino Real ("The Royal Road"), but it provided very slow passage between the Panamanian ports, and during heavy rainfalls its stones could not be seen because they were covered with piles of mud.

For nearly six weeks every year Porto Bello had a large trading fair where colonists and Spanish merchants exchanged goods. Products headed for Spain—mainly gold and silver from South American mines—were loaded onto cargo vessels at Porto Bello. These freighters were protected on their voyage across the Atlantic Ocean by warships from the Spanish fleet. Most of the Spanish products sold to Americans were transported across the isthmus to Panama City and then sent on ships to South American ports.

Officials of the Spanish government wished that a canal could be built in Panama. As early as 1529 Hernando Cortés, the conqueror of Mexico and much of Central America, wrote the Spanish king, Charles V, about the need for an Atlantic-Pacific canal. "We have not found as yet a passage [from Spain to China]," he said, "but we must cut it. No matter what cost, we must build a canal at Panama."[2]

The king ordered the governor of Panama to look into this possibility by having a survey made of the land through which a canal might be dug. The surveyors reported that such a waterway was not feasible because it seemed impossible to uproot the area's dense vegetation and cut through the mountains. Still, for the next thirty years, the Spanish continued to hope that somehow a canal could be constructed in Panama. Finally the king concluded that it was not "God's will" to have such a canal and that "if God had wanted a waterway across Panama, it would have been put there at the time of the Creation."[3]

In colonial times pirates frequently seized treasure-laden Spanish ships and raided Panama's rich trading ports. Henry Morgan and his band of English pirates completely destroyed Panama City in 1671. Before setting fire to the city's buildings, Morgan's men stripped them of all their valuable contents. But in one church a quick-thinking priest hurriedly painted a gold altar black. When the pirates saw the blackened altar, they thought it had no value and left it. Later the black paint was carefully rubbed off the gold altar, which was moved to another church.

The Spanish never tried to rebuild the ruined city. Instead, two years later they started constructing the present Panama City at a site about seven miles west of what is now called Old Panama.

CROSSING THE ISTHMUS

During the early 1800s the Spanish empire in the Americas crumbled. From Argentina in the south to Mexico in the north, people revolted against Spanish rule and declared their independence.

Panama won its freedom from Spain in 1821. Then it joined the new nation of Gran Colombia, a federation that also included modern-day Colombia, Venezuela, and Ecuador. After the confederation fell apart between 1828 and 1830, Panama became a province of Colombia. As the years passed, many Panamanians resented being governed by Colombia. Several times in the 1800s groups in Panama led revolts against Colombian rule, but their efforts were unsuccessful.

In 1823 United States President James Monroe had proclaimed a doctrine warning the European powers not to plant new colonies in the Western Hemisphere nor to interfere in the affairs of Latin American nations. The Monroe Doctrine became a cornerstone of the United States's foreign policy, but at the time it was announced the Americans were not militarily strong enough to enforce it. The doctrine did not prevent Great Britain from starting settlements in Nicaragua. Nor did it stop both the British and French from seriously considering the construction of a canal through either Panama or Nicaragua.

Since the United States was also interested in a Central American canal, it did not want any European country to gain a foothold in Panama. So U.S. diplomat Benjamin Bidlack was commissioned to seek a treaty with Colombia that would give his government special rights in the province of Panama. At that time the Colombians feared that the British might invade the defenseless isthmus, so they readily agreed to the Bidlack Treaty in 1846.

By this treaty the United States was given free transit across Panama along any road, railroad, or canal it might build. In exchange the United States agreed to protect the neutrality of the isthmus against any foreign invaders. It also promised to respect Colombia's sovereignty over Panama. (Sovereignty is the supreme power or authority to control and govern a territory.)

Events occurred in the United States in the 1840s that spurred interest in creating a faster passage between the Atlantic and Pacific Oceans. During this decade the United States gained possession of the Oregon Territory, and it acquired both California and the vast New Mexico Territory as a result of the Mexican War. Then, in 1848, gold was discovered in California.

Thousands of people from various parts of the United States began migrating to the West. Some crossed the country in slowly moving wagons. Others boarded ships on the Atlantic coast that sailed around the southern tip of South America and then up the Pacific coast to ports in California. This was a long, difficult journey. The swiftest trip from the East to the West was to sail southward in the Atlantic Ocean to Panama, cross the isthmus by mule train, and then take another ship headed northward in the Pacific Ocean.

Although it covered only a short distance, the trek across Panama's so-called Royal Road was fraught with hardships and dangers. Travelers had to contend with heat, humidity, torrential rains, piles of mud, bumpy rides on mules, poisonous snakes, and, worst of all, the usually fatal illnesses known as malaria, yellow fever, and cholera.

One young gold seeker who crossed the isthmus wrote to his family, "I say it in fear of God and love of man, to one and all, for no consideration [amount of money] come this route."[4]

A group of New York businessmen believed they could make a large profit by building a railroad across Panama. Construction was begun in 1850, and the railroad was completed five years later. The workers who hacked through the jungle growth and laid the tracks were mostly free black men from the West Indies.

Living conditions for these workers were miserable. About 9,000 laborers died, chiefly from yellow fever and malaria but also from cholera, dysentery, smallpox, and the effects of being overworked and underfed.

Construction of the Panama Railroad cost about $8 million; it was more expensive than any other railroad that covered such a short distance. During the first fourteen years after the track was laid, about 600,000 passengers rode the Panama Railroad, each paying twenty-five dollars for a one-way ticket. As much as $750 million in gold bullion from California crossed the isthmus on the railroad and then was shipped to ports in the eastern part of the United States. The railroad's owners reaped huge dividends from their investment.

THE FRENCH FAILURE

Meanwhile, the British had announced plans to construct an Atlantic-Pacific canal in Nicaragua. This infuriated government leaders in the United States, who charged that a British canal in any part of Central America would violate the Monroe Doctrine. As tension between the two countries escalated, Great Britain decided in 1850 to send a special agent, Sir Henry Bulwer, to Washington, D.C., to confer with Secretary of State John M. Clayton. Their meetings resulted in the Clayton-Bulwer Treaty, by which the United States and Great Britain pledged they would work as equal partners in jointly building any interoceanic canal in Central America. Both countries agreed that neither of them would fortify or seek exclusive control over such a waterway. And they promised that the canal would be open to ships of all nations on equal terms.

Neither the United States nor Great Britain first attempted to build the interoceanic canal. Instead, a French company was formed in 1879 to undertake the construction of a canal in Panama at an estimated cost of $214 million. The president of the French Panama Canal Company was Ferdinand de Lesseps, who had gained worldwide acclaim when he completed building the sea-level Suez Canal in Egypt in 1869. The French company signed an agreement with Colombia, paying that government $10 million for the right to build the canal in its province of Panama.

U.S. President Rutherford B. Hayes protested that the French proposal violated the Bidlack Treaty with Colombia. He angrily declared that the "policy of this country is [to have] a canal under American control" that would be "virtually a part of the coastline of the United States."[5] As a sign of his disapproval, the president sent some warships to Panamanian waters.

Colombian leaders said they disagreed with Hayes's interpretation of the Bidlack Treaty. They were eager to reap the rich dividends that would come to Colombia from the greatly increased trade and travel provided by a canal. So the Colombians encouraged de Lesseps to begin digging.

The project would be enormously expensive, but large

numbers of French citizens agreed to buy stock in the canal-building company. They were told they would receive substantial profits from the fees to be charged to ships using the waterway. The French government leaders applauded these investments as acts of patriotism that would bring glory and great prestige to their homeland.

De Lesseps intended to build a sea-level waterway, similar to the Suez Canal. But his engineers told him that creating a canal in Panama with its mountainous terrain was much different from constructing a waterway across the flat desert land of Egypt. They urged him to equip the canal with a multitiered lock system. (Locks are something like giant steps. They are sections of a waterway that are closed off with gates, in which ships in transit are raised or lowered to the level of the next lock by raising or lowering the water level of that section.)

Refusing to heed the advice of his engineers, de Lesseps insisted on building a sea-level canal that would run along a flat plane from one ocean to the other. He said that the area with the highest elevation, known as Culebra, was only about 300 feet above sea level, and he planned to cut a gorge through the low mountains there.

Work began on the canal in 1882. The labor force consisted mainly of blacks from the Caribbean Islands; West Indian immigration to Panama in the 1880s reached a total of about 50,000. Smaller numbers of French, Indians, Chinese, and Africans joined in the excavation.

From its beginning, the project was hampered by serious problems. During heavy rainfall the Chagres River near the canal site overflowed its banks and covered the land with thick layers of mud that trapped many workers and their machinery. When the men tried to dig into the Culebra mountainsides (they called this the Culebra Cut), devastating landslides occurred. Engineers were unable to find any way to prevent tons of rocks and mud from crashing down and filling the newly dug holes below.

The French attempt to build the canal resulted in a loss of life that was staggering. It was estimated that yellow fever, malaria, other diseases, and accidents on the job killed between 16,000 and 22,000 workers. Many Frenchmen wrote their wills before leaving for Panama; a few had the foresight to bring their coffins with them. "It did not [make] any difference whether they were black or white," observed one worker bitterly. "They die[d] like animals."[6]

By the end of 1888 the French Panama Canal Company had run out of money and was facing bankruptcy. A large portion of the canal still had not been completed after seven years of hard physical labor.

De Lesseps finally abandoned the venture in 1889, but this was not the end of his problems. French courts found him and several associates guilty of fraud and bribery in raising funds for the waterway, but the verdict against de Lesseps was overturned on a technicality. Thousands of French families lost their life savings when their investments in the canal were wiped out, and the "Panamanian scandal" was so severe that it rocked the foundation of the French government.

De Lesseps died in 1894 at the age of eighty-nine. According to one historian this reclusive old man apparently "never fully understood how and why the company he had founded spun apart, taking with it a government of France, a sense of national honor, and the confidence in public institutions of an entire generation of French citizens. In his eulogies no one spoke of Panama."[7]

A new canal company was started in France in 1894, but it had great difficulty raising funds. In a halfhearted manner, it continued to work on the waterway until a buyer could be found to pay it for the equipment at the canal site, the portion of the canal that had been dug, and the rights obtained from Colombia to develop the project.

The French people's dream of constructing the water path across the isthmus ended in a dreadful nightmare. If the job was ever to be done, someone else would have to do it.

Each of these men played a significant role in the development of the Panama Canal: Philippe Bunau-Varilla (upper left), *John Hay* (upper right), *and Theodore Roosevelt* (lower left).

3

~ ~ ~

THE UNITED STATES BECOMES INVOLVED

By the beginning of the twentieth century the United States had become an imperialist nation. As a result of the Spanish-American War in 1898, the United States had acquired the Philippine Islands and Guam in the Pacific Ocean and Puerto Rico in the Caribbean Sea. The same war freed Cuba from Spain, and the United States assumed the role of guardian to this new island nation. Also in 1898 the American flag was planted in Hawaii, thus ending the long period when this chain of islands was ruled by native kings and queens.

THE NEED FOR A CANAL

During the Spanish-American War the United States Navy sent the battleship *Oregon* from San Francisco to Cuba. The *Oregon* had to sail nearly 13,000 miles around the tip of

South America. If there had been a Central American canal joining the Pacific to the Atlantic, the battleship's trip would have been shortened to only about 4,600 miles.

The lengthy voyage of the *Oregon* showed that a waterway through Central America was vital to both the defense and the commerce of the United States. Without such a waterway American naval and merchant ships were severely handicapped just at the time when the United States began flexing its military muscle and demanding recognition as a first-rate world power. President Theodore Roosevelt stressed the importance of an interoceanic canal in his first message to Congress in 1901. "No single great material work which remains to be undertaken on this continent is of such consequence to the American people," Roosevelt declared.[1]

The president and Congress wanted a United States–owned canal, but difficult obstacles lay in the way of achieving this goal. The Clayton-Bulwer Treaty of 1850 still bound the United States to work with Great Britain in jointly constructing a canal. If the canal extended through Panama, financial arrangements had to be made with the French New Panama Canal Company to compensate it for its machinery and equipment, the portion of the canal it had already completed, and the money it had paid Colombia for the rights to dig a canal on its land. Because the rights to build a canal could not be transferred from the French company to the United States without Colombia's permission, the United States would have to make a separate deal with Colombia for canal rights in Panama.

WHERE TO BUILD?

A major question to be resolved was whether the Central American canal should be built in Nicaragua or Panama. The Nicaraguan route had several advantages. Much of

Nicaragua could already be crossed by water. The San Juan River in the southeastern corner of the country stretched from the Caribbean Sea to large Lake Nicaragua. Between Lake Nicaragua and the Pacific Ocean lay a narrow strip of land extending only about thirteen miles. No highland areas—like Culebra in Panama—hindered the path of a canal in Nicaragua.

From a political standpoint Nicaragua offered another advantage. Unlike Panama, it was an independent country capable of making its own deal for a canal. Several official U.S. commissions between 1876 and 1901 recommended Nicaragua as the nation that could provide the cheapest and most efficient canal route.

On the other hand, a canal in Panama would be about 135 miles shorter than a canal in Nicaragua. This was of great importance to both the canal diggers and the shippers who would use the waterway. The time required by steamships to move through a Panama canal would be less than half the time needed in Nicaragua. Also, the Panama route was straighter. Panama was blessed with better deep-water harbors and an operating railroad near the canal site. Another factor in Panama's favor was that a canal across the short isthmus would cost less to operate.

Before the canal site could be selected, the United States wanted Great Britain to agree to end the Clayton-Bulwer Treaty and permit the United States alone to build, operate, and fortify the Central American waterway. At an earlier time the British probably would have rejected this proposal, but in 1900 they were deeply involved in the Boer War in South Africa and were becoming concerned about Germany's growing strength in Europe. So the British government was willing to abandon some of the projects it had planned in other parts of the world, including Central America.

In early 1900 Secretary of State John Hay and Julian

Pauncefote, the British ambassador in Washington, D.C., signed a treaty that permitted the United States to build and own—but not fortify—an Atlantic-Pacific waterway. The Senate rejected the treaty because Hay had not also obtained the right of the United States to fortify the canal.

The secretary of state was furious with the Senate and with Democratic presidential nominee William Jennings Bryan, who led the opposition to the treaty. Writing to a friend, Hay said that Bryan struck at the treaty "in mere ignorance and malice, as an idiot might strike at a statue because he happened to have a hammer in his hand."[2]

Hay had to reopen the negotiations and finally won from the British the concession that Americans would have the right to fortify the canal. The second Hay-Pauncefote Treaty was signed in November 1901 and ratified by the Senate. By this treaty the United States promised to keep the canal open to ships of all nations in times of peace and to charge an equal fee to all vessels using the water passage.

When the members of Congress hotly debated the Nicaragua-versus-Panama canal site, a wily foreigner lobbied strenuously for the Panama route. He was Philippe Bunau-Varilla, a French engineer and major stockholder in the nearly defunct French New Panama Canal Company. He was eager to sell that company's concessions in Panama to the United States. The original asking price was $109 million, but when government officials said that the United States would pay no more than $40 million for the French holdings, Bunau-Varilla and his associates dropped the price to this figure.

There still were many supporters of the Nicaragua route in Congress, and Bunau-Varilla worked tirelessly to change their minds. By coincidence, acts of nature suddenly boosted the Frenchman's cause. On May 8, 1902, Mount Pelée, an enormous, long-dormant volcano on the West Indian island of Martinique, erupted. Killing nearly 30,000 people, this eruption was one of history's worst natural disasters. Then a few days later Momotombo, a volcano in Nicaragua, also erupted. It did little damage and was about a hundred miles from the proposed canal line, but this event gave Bunau-Varilla a clever idea.

He remembered seeing a Nicaraguan postage stamp that showed a railroad wharf in the foreground and, in the background, Momotombo erupting. Rushing about to every stamp dealer in Washington, Bunau-Varilla was able to purchase ninety of these stamps, one for each senator. He pasted each stamp on a sheet of paper and below each typed this message: "An official witness of the volcanic activity on the isthmus of Nicaragua."[3] The stamps arrived at the offices of every senator three days before the deciding vote. Since Panama had a history of freedom from volcanic eruptions, the Nicaraguan stamps may have influenced some wavering senators.

After fourteen days of debate, the Senate vote came on June 19. Forty-two senators voted for the Panama site and thirty-four senators for the Nicaragua site. The House of Representatives also approved the Panama route. But one important hurdle still had to be cleared before digging in Panama could begin: Colombia had to permit the United States to construct the canal on its soil.

The secretary of state began negotiations with Dr. Tomás Herrán, a Colombian diplomat. Their talks ended successfully in January 1903 with the signing of the Hay-Herrán Treaty. It granted the United States a strip of land six miles wide along the general route that de Lesseps had originally proposed for the canal. In return the United States agreed to pay Colombia $10 million, plus $250,000 annual rent for the canal zone.

The U.S. Senate ratified the Hay-Herrán Treaty. However, the senate of the Colombian government, meeting in the capital city of Bogotá, rejected the treaty by a unanimous vote. The Isthmus of Panama was regarded as one of Colombia's most valuable natural assets, and the Colombian senators felt that their country was not getting enough money for its use. They pointed out that the United States had promised to pay the French canal company represented by Philippe Bunau-Varilla $40 million for French concessions in Panama, but it was willing to pay only one-fourth this amount to Colombia, which owned the isthmus. Evidence later discovered indicated that if Colombia had been offered an additional $15 million, the pact would have been approved.

Theodore Roosevelt was infuriated when he received word from Bogotá that the Colombians had turned down the treaty. "I do not think," the president said, "that the Bogotá lot of jack rabbits should be allowed permanently to bar one of the future highways of civilization."[4]

PANAMANIAN INDEPENDENCE

Crestfallen by Colombia's decision and fearing that his $40 million deal with the United States was about to collapse, Bunau-Varilla realized that his only hope now was to help start a revolt in Panama. The Panamanians, eager to escape Colombian rule, needed little encouragement. Five times between 1846 and 1899 they had unsuccessfully tried to break away from Colombia. Another attempt occurred in 1901–1902, and peace was finally restored through the mediation of U.S. naval officers.

Bunau-Varilla got in touch with a group of prominent Panamanians who were plotting still another uprising against Colombia. The leader of the group was Manuel Amador Guerrero, who was commissioned to find out how the U.S. authorities would react if the Panamanians sought their freedom. Amador sailed to the United States, where he held meetings with Bunau-Varilla, who was in close contact with President Roosevelt and Secretary of State Hay. Bunau-Varilla convinced Amador that the U.S. government would look favorably upon a revolt and would protect an independent Panama.

Before Amador returned to Panama, Bunau-Varilla supplied him with a ready-made revolution kit. It contained a proclamation of independence, a military plan, the draft of a constitution, a code by which he and the rebels could communicate, a national flag, and even the date—November 3—for the revolution to commence. All that Bunau-Varilla asked in return was that he be appointed Panama's official representative in Washington to draft the future canal treaty. Amador agreed to this request.

On November 3, 1903—just as Bunau-Varilla had predicted—the revolt in Panama began. The United States government supplied the military muscle for the Panamanian rebels. The *Nashville,* a U.S. gunboat, arrived in the Caribbean port of Colón the day before the revolt. Other warships were sent to Panama City. The Panama Railroad was ordered not to transport Colombian troops across the isthmus.

When a small number of Colombian troops tried to move from Colón to Panama City, American naval officers stopped them. The Colombians were told that the rights given to the United States under the 1846 Bidlack Treaty, which guaranteed the freedom of passage across the isthmus, could not be endangered by any fighting. This was an almost comical ruse, since the Bidlack Treaty was not intended to be used against Colombia, which owned Panama and with which the United States had made the pact.

Panama gained its freedom within three days. The only

casualties occurred when a Colombian gunboat briefly opened fire, shooting five or six shells into Panama City and killing a Chinese shopkeeper and a donkey. The Panamanians declared their country's independence on November 6; on the same day the United States formally recognized the new republic.

Amador was proclaimed acting president, and a huge crowd cheered when the nation's flag was raised at Cathedral Plaza in Panama City. "Yesterday we were but the slaves of Colombia; today we are free," exclaimed Amador. Then he paid tribute to the United States and its president for making this possible. "President Roosevelt has made good. . . . Long live President Roosevelt! Long live the American government!"[5]

On November 18, 1903, Secretary of State Hay and Bunau-Varilla, representing Panama, signed the treaty that paved the way not only for the canal, but also for more than seventy years of strained relations between Panama and the United States. It gave the United States the right to construct a canal in Panama through a zone ten miles in width (in contrast to a zone of six miles in the Hay-Herrán Treaty). This area was called the Panama Canal Zone. Geographically, Panama City and Colón lay within the zone's boundaries, but the 1903 treaty stipulated that they were not to be considered part of the Panama Canal Zone. However, the water supply, sewerage, sanitation, and maintenance of public order in these cities were placed under United States control.

The Hay–Bunau-Varilla Treaty also gave the United States four small islands in the Bay of Panama and the right to take over any other land or water areas "necessary and convenient" for the construction, operation, sanitation, or defense of the canal. The use, occupation, and control of the Panama Canal Zone by the United States was to continue "in perpetuity" (forever).

In return the United States pledged to guarantee the independence of Panama and protect it against any enemies. The United States paid Panama $10 million for the right to build the canal and agreed to additional $250,000 annual payments that would begin nine years later, when the canal was expected to be completed.

The terms of the treaty were extremely favorable to the United States and extremely unfavorable to Panama. But no Panamanian had signed the treaty or even been consulted about what it would contain. Instead Bunau-Varilla, a Frenchman, and the U.S. government sealed Panama's fate for many years to come. President Roosevelt would later remark, "I took Panama because Bunau-Varilla brought it to me on a silver platter."[6]

Amador and Federico Boyd, another Panamanian leader, were stunned when they met Bunau-Varilla at the Washington railroad station and were shown the treaty. It was reported that Amador fainted when he read the document and that Boyd slapped the Frenchman in his face. When these Panamanian patriots told Bunau-Varilla that the treaty terms were outrageous, he replied that if Panama rejected them, the United States would withdraw its protection of their new government and build the canal in Nicaragua. Reluctantly the founding fathers of Panama realized that they had to accept the despised treaty provisions or risk losing their country's freedom. Having achieved his goal, Bunau-Varilla resigned his position as Panama's representative in Washington, D.C., a week after he signed the canal treaty.

Colombia was infuriated because the United States had prevented it from putting down a revolution in one of its own provinces. Charges that the United States had acted as a ruthless bully toward a weaker neighbor echoed throughout Latin America. Leading newspapers in the United States sharply assailed President Roosevelt's actions, describing them as "gunboat diplomacy" and a "rough-riding assault upon another republic."[7]

Roosevelt, however, was not daunted by such criticism. In 1911, two years after he had left the presidency, he boasted to a California audience, "I took the isthmus, started the canal and then left Congress not to debate the canal, but to debate me."[8]

Theodore Roosevelt believed that the role he had played in Panama's affairs was one of the crowning achievements of his presidential administration. Most U.S. citizens agreed with their president.

THROUGH THE CANAL

When the Panama Canal was completed in 1914, English writer James Bryce said that this astounding project represented "the greatest liberty Man has ever taken with Nature."[9] To people living in 1914 the canal provided the same feelings of awe and excitement that people experienced in 1969 when the astronauts first landed on the moon. Constructing the Panama Canal remains to this day one of history's greatest engineering accomplishments.

Perhaps the best way to appreciate the enormity of this feat is first to understand what occurs when a ship crosses the isthmus through the canal. The fifty-mile trip of a ship traveling from the Atlantic Ocean to the Pacific Ocean begins in Limon Bay at the port of Cristóbal. Colón lies nearby, but since Colón is not considered a part of the Canal Zone, a new port town was started at Cristóbal. (At the Pacific end of the canal, another new port town, Balboa, was built.) Then the ship sails about seven miles in a channel that was cut through the Chagres River valley.

The channel ends at the Gatun locks. These three locks,

rising one after another, form a huge staircase that lift every ship about 85 feet from sea level to the level of Gatun Lake. Each of these giant concrete sea chambers is approximately 1,000 feet long, 70 feet deep, and 110 feet wide. A single lock can hold about 66 million gallons of water.

Cables are fastened to each ship as it enters a lock. These cables are then attached to small electric locomotives called mules that run atop both walls of the lock. The locomotives help pull the vessel into place and prevent it from smashing into one of the side walls.

At first the water in the lock is the same level as the channel from which the ship has just moved. After the gates are closed behind the ship, valves are opened that permit millions of gallons of water from Gatun Lake to flow into the lock through openings in the bottom of the chamber. Within a few minutes the rising water lifts the ship to the level of the next lock. Then the front gates are opened, and the vessel is pulled by the locomotives into the second lock. Once again water is pumped in, and the ship is raised to the height of the third lock. When the vessel leaves the third lock, it has climbed 85 feet and is ready to enter Gatun Lake.

The creation of Gatun Lake—the largest artificial lake in the world—meant that approximately 164 square miles of jungle vanished under water. Before the lake could be formed, a giant dam was constructed to harness the raging waters of the Chagres River. As water from the dam flowed into the lake, the tops of hills that were not completely covered emerged as small islands. Many animals and insects sought refuge on these islands. The largest island, Barro Colorado, later was designated a natural reservation for scientific research. It has at least seventy species of animals and many types of reptiles, spiders, and plant life.

The trip across Gatun Lake covers about twenty-two

miles. Then the ship approaches the channel known as the Gaillard Cut. Formerly called the Culebra Cut, it was renamed to honor Col. David D. Gaillard, the army engineer who was in charge of its construction. The Gaillard Cut runs between high hills. When it was excavated—first by the French company and later by the Americans—digging the channel triggered frequent mud slides and avalanches of falling rocks. Earth slides still continue today, especially during the rainy season, and dredges are kept busy clearing the channel. In some years as much as 1 million cubic yards of dirt and rocks are removed from this part of the canal.

After its eight-mile passage through the Gaillard Cut, the ship reaches the Pedro Miguel locks (one lock each for vessels headed in opposite directions). The lock lowers the vessel about thirty-one feet to Miraflores Lake. Once the ship crosses this mile-long lake, it is lowered by two Miraflores locks to the level of the Pacific Ocean. Less than ten miles away is the port town of Balboa and the Pacific's deep water. The entire journey through the Panama Canal usually takes about eight hours.

DIGGING, DISEASE, AND DEATH

The labor force needed to construct the canal came from all parts of the world—from ninety-seven countries, according to the official records. Most of the engineers, skilled workers, and clerical staff came from the United States. The many unskilled pick-and-shovel men were mainly blacks from the islands in the West Indies. When de Lesseps had attempted to build the canal, Jamaica supplied the most workers. But the island of Barbados provided the largest number of laborers for the American-built waterway. Jamaican government officials, remembering the suffering endured by their people who had worked for de Lesseps, refused any recruiting by

Americans on their island and imposed a tax on Jamaicans who left to take canal jobs.

At the height of construction the canal project had between 43,000 and 50,000 people working at the same time. But there was a huge turnover in the labor force; perhaps as many as 250,000 people worked on the canal at one time or another. This turnover resulted mainly from poor living and working conditions; low pay; the hot, humid climate; and, especially during the first stages of construction, the horrible fear of contracting life-threatening tropical diseases. Mainly because of the lack of proper sanitation, yellow fever and malaria, which had struck down many of de Lesseps's employees, still ravaged the Canal Zone. President Roosevelt was aware of this deplorable situation. "The sanitary and hygienic problems," he said, "are those which are literally of the first importance, coming even before the engineering."[10]

U.S. Army Medical Corps officer Col. William C. Gorgas was put in charge of the campaign against yellow fever and malaria. He had been part of the team of army doctors who had wiped out yellow fever in Cuba following the Spanish-American War. These doctors had discovered that yellow fever was transmitted by the *Aedes* mosquito.

Gorgas attacked the mosquito's breeding grounds. He knew that the female mosquito deposited her eggs only in standing water, such as could be found in rain barrels and ponds. Gorgas ordered that all water containers be covered with lids. He had ponds, swamps, and streams drained. If all the standing water could not be drained away, it was sprayed with a layer of oil to prevent the female from laying her eggs in the water and to kill any eggs and larvae (insects hatched from the eggs). Some buildings were fumigated, and screens were put on the doors and windows of the buildings in the Canal Zone.

By 1906 Gorgas and his assistants had won the war

against yellow fever in Panama. Malaria, carried by a different mosquito, was harder to combat because the female laid her eggs in many other places besides standing water. But by 1914 sanitation measures and improved medical practices had greatly reduced the number of deaths from this dreaded disease.

At first construction on the canal proceeded slowly. It was June 1906 before both houses of Congress voted in favor of using locks rather than building a sea-level canal. Haggling and indecision on the part of government officials both in Washington and in the Canal Zone delayed the project. Both the first and the second civilian engineers selected to serve as the canal's chief engineer became frustrated and resigned. Finally, in 1907, President Roosevelt turned to the U.S. Army Corps of Engineers and appointed Col. George W. Goethals to head the project.

Goethals was determined to apply military discipline and efficiency to his new job. "I now consider that I am commanding the Army of Panama," he declared, "and that the enemy we are going to combat is the Culebra Cut and the locks and dams at both ends of the Canal."[11] His firm leadership and wise decisions accelerated the difficult construction of the giant waterway.

On August 15, 1914, the S.S. *Ancon*, a cement carrier, made the first official passage through the Panama Canal. Since that time many thousands of commercial and military ships have used the "big ditch" to move between the oceans. About 12,000 vessels pass through the canal yearly, and many of these ships are traveling to or from U.S. ports.

The collection of tolls is an important function of the canal operators; these tolls help pay the expenses incurred in the Canal Zone. Congress decreed in 1914 that all merchant ships, including those from the United States, must pay a toll that is determined by the number of tons of cargo they are carrying. Tolls on military ships are based on their weight.

In 1988 the huge British liner *Queen Elizabeth II* paid a record-setting toll—$106,783. The lowest toll on record was paid by Richard Halliburton, a famous adventurer. In 1928 this 140-pound man paid a toll of thirty-six cents for the privilege of swimming through the Panama Canal.

Panamanians felt strongly that their flag should
fly along with the U.S. flag in the Canal Zone.

4

~ ~ ~

DAYS OF DISCORD, YEARS OF TENSION

Two parallel governments arose in Panama following independence, one for the republic (under American protection) and another for the Canal Zone. The republic of Panama had the outward appearance of a nation-state, but its powers were severely restricted by the United States. The British minister to Panama wrote in 1910, "It is really farcical to talk of Panama as an independent state. It is really simply an annex of the Canal Zone."[1]

SOVEREIGNTY WITHOUT POWER

The 1903 Hay–Bunau-Varilla Treaty stripped Panama of all its rights to govern—its sovereignty—in the Canal Zone. Secretary of State Hay declared that Article 3 of the treaty granted to the United States "all the rights, power, and authority . . . which the United States would possess if it were the sovereign . . . to the entire exclusion of the exercise by the Republic of Panama of any such sovereign rights, power and authority."[2]

In an attempt to appease the Panamanians, Hay acknowledged that Panama retained "titular sovereignty" (sovereignty in name only) in the Canal Zone. That is to say, the United States recognized that Panama had a nominal title to the zone, without any duties or powers and, if the United States ever withdrew, the territory would be returned to Panama.

This interpretation of the 1903 treaty promoted fierce anti-American feelings among the people of Panama. What was sovereignty, they asked, without any sovereign powers? How could the Canal Zone be considered part of their country if neither the government nor the Panamanian people had any rights there? Or any prospect of ever receiving such rights, since the treaty stated that its provisions were to last forever? The Panamanians' interpretation of the treaty was that the Americans were entitled to sovereign authority only in matters related to the construction, maintenance, and protection of the canal.

DISPUTE AND TENSION

The natives of Panama also objected to the treaty provision that permitted the United States to take additional lands outside the Canal Zone if it believed they were needed for the defense of the canal. They argued that Panama already was a small country divided into two smaller sections by the Canal Zone and that the United States should not have the right to take over even more of its land. The slogan "Land Divided, World United" was not popular with Panamanians.

The United States, on the other hand, insisted that this treaty provision was just and reasonable. After all, the American government had provided the money, machinery, and engineering skills needed to construct and operate the canal. Since this project represented a huge investment, it had to be protected against possible foreign foes and local rebellions, so additional bases might be required for its defense. On much the same grounds, the United States upheld its right, according to the 1903 treaty, to "maintain public order" in Colón and Panama City, even though these cities were not considered part of the Canal Zone.

An important phase of U.S. rule in the Canal Zone was the administration of justice. Congress could and did pass laws that pertained to this area. Its inhabitants, known as Zonians, were subject to the laws of the United States, to arrest by United States police, and to trial by United States judges. Yet it seemed wrong to Panamanian Zonians that while living in territory they felt belonged to them they should be tried by foreigners under foreign laws.

The discrimination practiced in the Canal Zone was also resented by many of the people who lived there. It began while the canal was being constructed and continued for many years afterward. Housing, cafeterias, schools, and hospitalization were separate and by no means equal. There were even two sets of rest rooms and drinking fountains: one for American and European whites and the other for everyone else.

Whites were paid in gold, which was then the monetary standard of the United States. All other employees were paid in Panama's silver pesos, worth less than half as much as gold payments. Canal authorities avoided using the term *white* for one group and *black and mestizo* for the other group. Instead, for payroll purposes the whites were classified as "gold" and minorities as "silver." The "silver" employees hated this form of discrimination, which defied the principle of equal pay for equal work.

Another source of antagonism between Panamanians and Americans pertained to the commissaries (stores) in the Canal Zone. From the early days of canal construction, commissaries were operated in the zone by the U.S. government for the benefit of canal employees. Nearly all of the goods sold in these commissaries were imported from the United States. This practice infuriated merchants in Panama, who claimed that it was denying them the economic gains that could come from selling their products to the Zonians.

The government of Panama vigorously protested that it was not receiving a large enough amount of money from the profits produced by the operation of the canal. It demanded from the United States higher annuities—the annual payment of rent for the Canal Zone—and also a fair share of the tolls collected from the ships using the waterway.

In time most of the Panamanian-American differences were resolved in Panama's favor. But it took many years—and occasionally blood was shed—before these differences were successfully negotiated.

In 1914, the year that the canal was completed, World War I began in Europe. The United States recognized the strategic value of the canal as a means for swift transfer of warships and as a naval base in the protection of the Caribbean sea-lanes. Shortly after the United States entered the war in 1917, Panama also declared war on Germany. Some Panamanian nationalists opposed this action, fearing that their little country had been pulled into an international conflict on behalf of an unwanted guardian.

During the war the United States exercised its protective rights against German citizens living in Panama. They were interned in camps, and the government of Panama cooperated with the United States in an effort to prevent sabotage by enemy sympathizers.

In the midst of the war American oil companies were first established in Panama, outside the Canal Zone. The arrival of additional Americans on their soil infuriated Panamanians. Demonstrations occurred, and clashes between Americans and the local people grew sufficiently dangerous to warrant the sending of armed forces from the United States. American marines arrived in the province of Chiriquí in July 1918, and they remained there for two years.

Later Panama and Costa Rica disputed some borderland in the Coto district on the Pacific side of the isthmus. Both countries agreed to submit the dispute to arbitration by Chief Justice Edward White of the United States Supreme Court. The chief justice announced that the territory belonged to Costa Rica, but the Panamanians refused to surrender it. In 1921 Costa Rican troops seized the land. Then armed fighters from Panama moved in and temporarily regained the disputed territory. With both countries preparing for war, U.S. marines landed in Panama and forced that country to comply with the chief justice's decision and return the land to Costa Rica.

Secretary of State Charles Evans Hughes justified U.S. intervention in Panama's boundary controversy. He explained that since Panama had virtually no sovereignty, "the government of the United States deems it necessary to inquire fully into the merits of a controversy which relates to the boundary of the Republic of Panama."[3]

Trouble broke out again in 1925 when Panamanians revolted against the high rents they had to pay for housing in Panama City. Six hundred U.S. troops broke up a mob that was trying to take over Panama's capital city. This use of troops was taken in compliance with the clause in the 1903 treaty that permitted the United States to take steps in order to "maintain public order" in Panama City. However, this action fanned the anger of the people of Panama against their powerful neighbor to the north. Their hatred of American interference in local affairs was expressed violently when Gen. John J. Pershing, commander of U.S. armed forces in World War I, paid a ceremonial visit to Panama in 1925. The car in which Pershing was riding was stoned by an unruly crowd in Panama City.

THE UNITED STATES CHANGES ITS TUNE

The icy relations between Panama and the United States started to thaw in the presidential administration of Herbert Hoover. In 1929, between his election and inauguration, Hoover visited some South American nations. There he was told that most Latin Americans regarded the United States as an unfriendly imperialist power—the Colossus of the North—that frequently interfered in the affairs of its weaker neighbors. A short time later President Hoover announced that the United States would adopt a new policy of nonintervention in the internal affairs of Latin American nations.

The first time that this new policy was applied to Panama occurred in 1931. A militant political organization called Acción Communal led a rebellion that unseated the Panamanian president and replaced him with one of its members, Harmodio Arias. The opinions openly expressed by Arias were strongly anti-American, and he threatened to defy many of the provisions of the 1903 treaty. But the United States government made no effort to remove him from office.

When Franklin D. Roosevelt became president of the United States in 1933, he promised to continue Hoover's commitment that the United States would not intervene in the domestic affairs of Latin American countries. In his inaugural address President Roosevelt declared, "In the field of world policy I would dedicate this nation to the policy of a good neighbor—the neighbor who resolutely respects himself, and, because he does so, respects the rights of others."[4]

The Good Neighbor Policy was applied to Panama in a treaty signed in 1936. Among the chief elements of this treaty were elimination of the concept that Panama was a protectorate of the United States, an increase in the annuity paid each year to Panama for use of the Canal Zone from $250,000 to $430,000, and the promise not to take any additional land for military bases without the permission of the Panamanian government. This treaty was not ratified by the U.S. Senate until 1939 because many senators insisted that it gave too many concessions to Panama.

DEFENDING THE CANAL IN WORLD WAR II

In 1940 Arnulfo Arias (the brother of Harmodio Arias) was elected president of Panama. At that time Adolf Hitler's German war machine had seized much of Western Europe and was threatening Great Britain and the Soviet Union. It was feared that the Panama Canal was included in Hitler's conquest plans. However, President Arias refused to permit the United States to have free access to land for bases that would help protect his country and its canal. Under no circumstances did he wish to appear as a puppet of the Yankees, and he was determined to preserve his nation's neutrality if the United States went to war.

The State Department presented Arias with a list of defense sites to be used for air bases, antiaircraft artillery, communication stations, and radar equipment. Arias evidently assumed that the United States would pay any price for these sites and demanded a $25 million program of benefits for Panama plus a fifty-year prepayment of the annuity, which totaled $21.5 million. U.S. officials turned down this extravagant demand.

Soon, however, Arias faced serious trouble from his own people. While he claimed to be neutral in the world conflict, he encouraged German propagandists to fill Panama's newspapers with pro-German stories, exiled pro-U.S. journalists, and conferred Panamanian citizenship on Germans and Italians residing in his country (Italy was an ally of Germany in World War II). In nearby Colombia Germans had helped to found the national airline, which employed German pilots, whose planes were within easy striking distance of Panama. While many Panamanians were not strong admirers of the United States, they blamed Arias for refusing to cooperate with the only country that could help defend them against air and naval attacks from German forces. Also, Arias was unpopular because he had imposed severe measures against Panama's West Indians and their descendants, whose citizenship, jobs, and civil rights were put in jeopardy.

In 1941 Arias was overthrown by Panama's National Guard, which served as the nation's military and police force. Ricardo de la Guardia was installed as the new president. He was a political moderate and much friendlier to the United States than Arias had been.

When Japanese airplanes bombed Pearl Harbor on December 7, 1941, the United States went to war against Japan, Germany, and Italy, known as the Axis powers. Panama also declared war on the Axis countries, and President de la Guardia offered full military cooperation to the United States. Americans were given temporary use of the sites needed for defense bases, with the understanding that they would be returned to Panama within a year after World War II ended. The U.S. government then established 134 bases of various military types on Panama's soil.

Tight security measures were imposed during the war.

Letters and cablegrams were censored, and the Panamanian government cooperated with U.S. officials in detaining over 1,200 citizens of the Axis nations. After they had been screened, most of these persons were freed, but 327 of them were classified as potential security risks capable of committing sabotage. They were sent to internment camps in the United States.

Seventy thousand American military personnel were stationed on the isthmus to protect the canal. The importance of the canal during the war cannot be overestimated. It provided a speedy Atlantic-Pacific passage for many warships, troopships, and cargo vessels carrying weapons and other provisions. The Panama Canal helped make it possible for the United States to fight successfully against enemies both in Europe and in Asia.

A NEW TREATY

After the war ended, the United States handed back to Panama most of the base sites it had acquired since 1941. The Pentagon insisted, however, that some bases were still needed to protect the canal from possible attacks by future enemies, especially those who had nuclear weapons. Panamanian officials agreed in December 1947 to permit the United States to retain a number of strategic bases for a period of five years.

This action triggered violent anti-American demonstrations by the people of Panama. The riots led to the resignation of Panama's foreign minister, who had negotiated the bases agreement. The Panamanian National Assembly unanimously voted to reject the deal. Once again Panama returned to its prewar position of applying pressure to extract concessions from the United States.

The first significant opportunity for obtaining concessions came after Col. José Remón was elected president in 1952, the same year in which Gen. Dwight D. Eisenhower was elected president of the United States. Remón demanded that the United States agree to make revisions in the 1903 treaty, including changes that would improve his nation's economy. He wanted the United States to pay a higher annuity for use of the Canal Zone, share canal tolls with Panama, and provide equal pay for Panamanians and Americans working in the zone. Furthermore, Remón called for U.S. recognition of Panamanian sovereignty in the Canal Zone and equal display of the two countries' flags in the zone.

U.S. government officials indicated their willingness to meet with negotiators from Panama. In August 1953 Remón organized a giant rally to demonstrate public support for his negotiating team before it left for Washington. About 100,000 cheering people gathered at the rally; this was the most remarkable show of national unity in Panama's history.

One of the departing diplomats, Octavio Fabrega, told the huge crowd, "Fifty years of the Bunau-Varilla treason will soon be observed, fifty years in which the people of Panama have been under the yoke of an enslaving treaty. . . . Panama gave away . . . the treasure of its geographic position in that treaty. Panama has not received adequate compensation for the sacrifices it has made and is making here at the Canal."[5]

In September Remón traveled to Washington to seek President Eisenhower's personal support for treaty revisions. After a forty-minute meeting with Remón, Eisenhower told his aides that he would approve changes in U.S. relations with Panama, but only in areas that did not sacrifice vital U.S. interests.

After two years of negotiations the Eisenhower-Remón Treaty was signed in 1955 and later ratified by the United States Senate and the Panamanian National Assembly. The treaty raised the price of the yearly annuity to Panama from $430,000 to $1,930,000. It provided for an end to discrimination in Canal Zone employment and wages. The old gold and silver payrolls were abolished, and jobs at equal pay were opened in the zone to all qualified Panamanians, except for those positions related to safeguarding the canal.

The treaty also promised that the United States would build a bridge across the canal at the Pacific coast port of Balboa. The bridge would help lessen the complaint that the canal was dividing the country into two parts and making it difficult for people on one side of the waterway to do business with people on the other side. This bridge was completed in the early 1960s at a cost of about $20 million.

VIOLENCE DIVIDES THE TWO COUNTRIES

The U.S. treaty negotiators, however, refused to accept all of the Panamanians' demands. Nothing was included in the document about giving Panama sovereignty over the Canal Zone or the equal display of both nations' flags in the zone. And the Americans refused to share canal tolls with Panama, partly because sharing this revenue might imply sharing control of the canal, too.

Flying their flag in the Canal Zone was an emotional issue of great importance to the people of Panama. It would provide symbolic evidence that their country had titular sovereignty in the zone, even though this sovereignty was in name only.

On May 2, 1958, a group of students marched into the Canal Zone and planted seventy-two Panamanian flags on its grounds. Their motto was "Operation Sovereignty." Zone police quickly removed both the students and the flags.

Riots then occurred outside the zone, and the National Guard attacked the demonstrators, killing one of them and injuring others. The students responded with a defiant funeral march that led to more fighting. This bloodshed in 1958 marked the beginning of a dangerous, violent phase in U.S.-Panamanian relations. It was an omen of even more destructive demonstrations to come.

In August 1959 political leader Aquilino Boyd announced that on November 3 he and his followers would parade the Panamanian flag through the Canal Zone. November 3 was the anniversary of the founding of Panama, and Boyd's grandfather had been one of the founders. American authorities in the zone reacted negatively to this announcement. They had an eight-foot-high fence built along the border separating the canal from the downtown section of Panama City. After a wall was built in Berlin, East Germany, in 1961 to prevent communist East Berliners from entering democratic West Berlin, the people of Panama referred to the fence near the canal as "the little Berlin wall."

Early on November 3 a large group assembled on Fourth of July Avenue in Panama City. They asked permission to enter the Canal Zone with their flag, but their request was denied. Then some of the demonstrators crossed the avenue and tried to push their way into the zone. The police forced them to retreat. But when the Panamanian flag fell to the ground and was torn, tempers flared. Before order was restored, the angry mob struck the police with clubs, rocks, and bottles.

Meanwhile other sympathizers poured into the streets of Panama City and advanced on the U.S. embassy. Many of the embassy windows were broken, and the American flag was hauled from its pole and torn into pieces. The battle continued at another spot two miles away. The Panamanian National Guard and U.S. troops had to use tear gas to disperse a mob of about 300 rioters who pelted them with rocks and bottles.

In the tumult about forty persons were injured, but no one was killed. Less than a month later, however, new riots broke out and injured another eighteen people.

TURBULENT TIMES

The United States government added these bloody events in Panama to the series of serious foreign problems it faced in 1959. Relations with the Communist leaders of the Soviet Union continued to deteriorate, and the dreadful possibility of a war with nuclear weapons escalated. In Asia Communist China threatened to attack Taiwan, and Communist forces in North Vietnam were fighting to conquer South Vietnam. In the Western Hemisphere Fidel Castro had overthrown the government of Cuba in January 1959 and was moving his country in the direction of an alliance with the Soviet Union.

Inspired by Castro's use of guerrilla fighters to topple the Cuban government, three times in 1959 bands of insurgents led revolts in Panama. Their efforts failed, but U.S. officials became increasingly concerned that the riots and insurrections in Panama pointed a dagger at the valuable canal.

President Eisenhower tried to ease the poor relations with Panama by announcing in December 1959 that he believed "we should have visual evidence that Panama does have titular sovereignty" over the Canal Zone.[6] This meant that at least one Panamanian flag should be flown in the zone.

The president's announcement set off a wave of protests in the United States. Many Americans earnestly believed that the Panama Canal was virtually a U.S. possession. They argued that to display a "foreign" flag in recognition of titular sovereignty would generate future Panamanian demands for complete sovereignty. By a vote of 380 to 12, the House of

Representatives passed a resolution opposing the display of Panama's flag in the zone. Since this was only a resolution and not a congressional bill, it did not limit the president's authority to take whatever action he felt was proper. But the overwhelming size of the vote in the House reflected the public's strong disapproval of the flag plan.

Finally, on September 17, 1960, by executive order, President Eisenhower directed that the Panamanian flag be flown in the Canal Zone at Shaler Triangle, a highly visible plaza next to Panama City. The people of Panama applauded this action, but it fell far short of responding to all of their grievances. As one observer remarked, the Panama Canal is "a body of water completely surrounded by trouble."[7]

AID TO LATIN AMERICA

The presidency of John F. Kennedy, which began in 1961, brought new hope to Panamanian government leaders. Shortly after taking office, President Kennedy launched the Alliance for Progress, a program designed to aid all of Latin America. Billions of dollars were poured into Latin American countries, including Panama, to improve their people's housing, medical care, public utilities, education, roads and highways, and methods of farming. One purpose of the Alliance for Progress was to prevent the spread of communism by reducing poverty and poor living conditions. Another Kennedy project, the Peace Corps, sent American volunteers into underdeveloped countries, such as Panama, to help communities cope with a variety of problems.

Many Panamanians received aid from these programs, and President Roberto Chiari believed that the young, idealistic American president might take further steps to ease the strained relations between their two countries. In June 1962 Chiari flew to Washington and conferred with Kennedy for two days. Kennedy made no major concessions at their meetings, but he and Chiari agreed to appoint diplomats to continue discussions of the two nations' mutual problems.

One of the subjects Kennedy and Chiari talked about was whether a new sea-level canal (without locks) should be built, since the locks of the Panama Canal were too narrow for some large modern ships. Experts had suggested that both money and time could be saved if the builders of a sea-level canal used nuclear devices for excavation. (Later, in August 1963, the United States approved the Nuclear Test Ban Treaty, prohibiting nuclear explosions in the atmosphere, and this apparently ended the possibility of nuclear excavation of a sea-level canal.)

After the two presidents' talks ended, Kennedy signed a secret memorandum acknowledging that a new treaty with Panama would eventually be drafted, either to revise the 1903 treaty or to cover a sea-level canal. The American president also ordered that the Panamanian flag would fly alongside the Stars and Stripes at fifteen sites in the Canal Zone in addition to the Shaler Triangle.

RIOTS ERUPT OVER FLYING THE FLAG

A few weeks after President Kennedy was assassinated in November 1963, and while his successor, Lyndon B. Johnson, was getting settled into office, violence again erupted in the Canal Zone and also in the nearby cities. On January 7, 1964, some American students in the zone raised the U.S. flag in front of Balboa High School. This was in defiance of the order given by the zone's American governor that no flags were to be flown at any schools in the Canal Zone. On the next two days the Zonians continued to fly the Stars and Stripes at Balboa High School.

This infuriated Panamanian students, and on January 9,

while the American governor was away, a large group of them marched into the zone. Four of the young people carried their national flag, and others carried a large banner proclaiming in Spanish that Panama was sovereign in the Canal Zone. They proceeded to Balboa High School, determined to hoist their flag there. The chief of police explained that there was only one pole at the school and that the U.S. flag already was flying from it. The marchers demanded that it be lowered and replaced by their own flag.

A shouting match developed, followed by pushing, shoving, and fighting between the Panamanian and American students. In the scuffle the flag of Panama was torn and several students were injured. This incensed the Panamanians, who then overturned and burned American cars and set fire to some buildings in the zone.

The next morning President Chiari charged that Americans had been guilty of unwarranted aggression and suspended Panama's diplomatic relations with the United States. (They were not restored until the following April.)

News of the bloody clash reached Panama's cities, and soon thousands of citizens were trying to push into the Canal Zone. Police in the zone tried to hold them back with tear gas and riot sticks. As the tumult grew more ominous, U.S. troops were called in to restore order in the zone.

In the following days the rioting spread to Panama City and Colón. Mobs ransacked the corporate offices of several U.S. banks, the U.S. Information Agency building, the offices of Pan American Airlines and Braniff Airways, and also the Firestone and Goodyear tire plants.

At first the Panamanian National Guard took no action to subdue its people. President Chiari and the leaders of the National Guard were afraid that if they intervened, the hatred of the rioters might be turned against them. When it became evident that guardsmen were making no arrests, widespread looting of stores and shops occurred.

Finally, on January 13, the situation had become so desperate that the National Guard had to step in. It placed armed officers throughout the cities bordering the canal, and at last peace was restored. But the rioting had exacted a heavy toll. Twenty Panamanians—one of them a student—and four Americans had died in the fighting; hundreds more had been injured. Loss of property, mainly American-owned buildings, exceeded $2 million. The people of Panama believed that those who had died in the uprising were martyrs, and they renamed the street separating Panama City from the Canal Zone: what had been Fourth of July Avenue was changed to Avenue of the Martyrs.

William J. Jorden, former U.S. ambassador to Panama, said that "neither side fully recovered from the psychological wounds inflicted during those three and a half days of violence and bloodshed. They created a trauma that remained just beneath the surface of American-Panamanian relations for the next decade and a half."[8]

NO SOLUTION

Developments in Panama stunned President Johnson and other U.S. government officials. They realized that the canal was in imminent danger of being attacked and perhaps destroyed by frustrated Panamanians. On March 21, 1964, President Johnson declared he would seek a solution to the problems that existed between the two countries; this would be a solution "which recognizes the fair claims of Panama."[9]

On national television in December, Johnson announced that negotiations to replace the 1903 treaty with three new treaties would soon begin. One treaty would have both

Panama and the United States share in the operation of the canal. Another treaty would pledge the two countries to protect the canal, guarantee its neutrality, and permit the continued use of the military bases that the United States already had in Panama. The third treaty would authorize the United States to construct a sea-level canal that would be operated jointly, in the same way as the existing canal.

The president acted boldly when he made these far-reaching proposals. In the same month a Gallup poll revealed that, by a margin of six to one, the American public was opposed to the United States's conceding to Panama any control over the canal.

Nevertheless, serious negotiations began in January 1965 and continued into 1967. The two presidents initialed treaty drafts in June 1967, but these drafts were leaked to the press before either president could brief legislative leaders in his country.

The effect of the leaks was to give both Panamanians and Americans something to criticize. The idea of sharing in the operation and defense of the canal did not satisfy Panamanians, who stubbornly insisted on having complete sovereignty over the Canal Zone. They condemned the new treaties as a surrender to American imperialism and another example of the "rape of Panama." In the United States there were vehement objections to giving up any American rights in the Canal Zone. Opponents of the agreement strongly asserted that the zone was U.S. property and must be controlled only by Americans.

President Johnson was informed that there was no possibility of getting the treaties ratified by Panama's National Assembly. Rather than support a lost cause, he suspended the negotiations. There was another reason why the president was willing to postpone any action regarding Panama. By 1967 President Johnson had become very unpopular with a large segment of the American public because of his escalation of the Vietnam War. He did not want to add to his troubles at home by continuing to seek an agreement with Panama that many Americans, as well as Panamanians, opposed vehemently.

The collapse of the negotiations ended the talks with Panama while Johnson was president. When they resumed, Panama had a new and powerful leader—Omar Torrijos.

In August 1977 U.S. President Jimmy Carter (left)
and Panama's General Omar Torrijos (right) *signed
two important treaties dealing with the sovereignty
and defense of the Canal Zone.*

5

~ ~ ~

THE CARTER-TORRIJOS TREATIES

Born in 1929, the son of a schoolteacher, Omar Torrijos sought a military career. After studying at a military school in El Salvador, he was commissioned a second lieutenant in Panama's National Guard in 1952. Later he attended advanced military institutes in the United States, the Canal Zone, and Venezuela.

Torrijos acquired a reputation as a capable officer and outstanding military leader. Rising through the ranks quickly, he became a colonel and was given command of the large garrison in Chiriquí Province.

A CHANGE OF POWER

In 1968 Arnulfo Arias was elected president of Panama for the third time. Arias was popular with many voters but not with most officers in the National Guard. Two of his chief opponents in the guard were Torrijos and Major Boris Martínez.

Shortly after he assumed the presidency, Arias revealed his plan to replace some high military officials, including Martínez and Torrijos, with people he felt he could control. But Arias had made the mistake of conducting a shake-up of the senior officers of the National Guard before first ensuring himself of military support. On the night of October 11, 1968, Martínez, Torrijos, and some of their comrades staged a successful coup, overthrowing Arias only eleven days after his inauguration.

Torrijos elevated his own rank to brigadier general and became commander of the National Guard; Martínez became a colonel and the guard's chief of staff. Officially the new government was run by a junta (a group of military officers ruling a country after seizing power). Taking orders from Torrijos and Martínez, the ruling junta did not move the country in the direction of democracy. Instead it banned political parties and tightened government control over the media.

In February 1969 Torrijos removed Martínez from his high position in the guard. Later that same year Torrijos himself became the victim of an attempted coup. While he was traveling in Mexico, three guard officers seized power and declared Torrijos deposed. They claimed he had ruled as a dictator and trampled on his country's democratic institutions.

Torrijos immediately returned to Panama, landing in the small city of David. There he was met by an officer loyal to him, Manuel Antonio Noriega, who commanded a garrison that had about one-fifth of the guard soldiers. Noriega welcomed Torrijos back as the legitimate commander of the National Guard on December 16—a date that from then on was to be celebrated every year in Panama as Loyalty Day.

With Noriega's troops and his civilian supporters surrounding him, Torrijos formed a caravan to drive the two hundred miles to Panama City. All along the route Torrijos made speeches and urged those who heard him to join the procession. When he reached the capital, an estimated 10,000 cheering people accompanied him.

Leaders of the coup were arrested, and Torrijos was restored to power. To give the appearance of supporting Panama's constitution, which said that the country was to be led by a president, Torrijos appointed a close friend, Demetrio Lakas, to serve as president. But the real power to govern was retained by Torrijos. He approved the budget, appointed cabinet members and ambassadors, decided which laws the country needed, and directed foreign policy.

Torrijos consolidated his power base in 1970 and 1971. He appealed for support from the Panamanian people by promising them strong labor unions, higher wages, agrarian reforms, and improvements in the public health system, housing, and education. In 1972 he convoked a constitutional convention that wrote a charter naming him chief of state.

A CLEVER MOVE

As Torrijos gained in strength, he spoke out more adamantly for a new relationship with the United States—one that accepted Panama's demands for sovereignty over the Canal Zone, a larger role in the operation of the canal, and an equitable share of the profits from the canal.

In 1973 Torrijos developed a clever strategy designed to force the United States to make concessions to Panama. His foreign minister, Juan Antonio Tack, and his ambassador to the United Nations, Aquilino Boyd, convinced the United Nations Security Council to hold a meeting in Panama. The chief purpose of this meeting was to focus world attention on Panama's claim that it was not being treated fairly by the United States.

Torrijos addressed the Security Council and vehemently argued his country's position regarding the canal issues. Then Ambassador Boyd proposed a resolution that would satisfy Panama's demands. United States diplomats responded that Panama's resolution was too radical and did not recognize the legitimate U.S. concerns about the Canal Zone and the operation and protection of the canal.

When the Security Council voted on the resolution, there were thirteen yeas, one nay (the United States), and one country not voting (Great Britain). Because the United Nations charter had given the veto power to each of the Security Council's five permanent members—including the United States—the resolution was vetoed. This was only the third time that the United States had exercised its veto power in the Security Council.

Even though the resolution had not been adopted, Panamanians believed they had mobilized a large segment of international opinion against the United States. Foreign Minister Tack proclaimed, "The United States has vetoed Panama, but the world has vetoed the United States!"[1]

MORE TALK ABOUT A NEW TREATY

U.S. government officials grew fearful that the escalating tensions between the two countries could lead to violence that would endanger the canal. So, within two months after the Security Council meeting in Panama, President Richard M. Nixon gravely reported to Congress that the time had come to develop a better relationship with this Central American neighbor.

In 1974 the United States and Panama reached an agreement to begin discussing the terms that would be included in a new treaty. Among the ideas to be considered were joint management and defense of the waterway, recognition of Panama's sovereignty over the Canal Zone, a higher annual canal fee for Panama, and the promise that both nations would work together in the future should the canal be expanded or a second canal built.

The discussions dragged on for three years without arriving at any conclusions. One reason that the negotiations stalled was the fierce resentment many Americans expressed toward changing the role of the United States in Panama. A national poll showed that 78 percent of the American public opposed "surrendering" the canal to Panama. "The canal was a living example of American ability and American strength," said author Michael Barone. "For many voters, to abandon it was to abandon an important part of America."[2]

An important factor that influenced public opinion in the mid-1970s was that the United States had just emerged from the tragic Vietnam War. This was the only war that the U.S. ever lost, and the possibility of also retreating from Panama seemed to many Americans another sign that their nation's position in the world arena was becoming shamefully weak.

In 1976, when Ronald Reagan, the former governor of California, contested President Gerald Ford for the Republican presidential nomination, he made the Panama issue one of the centerpieces of his political campaign. Audiences applauded loudly when he declared, regarding the canal, "We bought it, we paid for it, it's ours, and we aren't going to give it away to some tinhorn dictator [Torrijos]."[3] Reagan lost his bid for the presidential nomination to Ford, and Ford was defeated in the general election by Democrat Jimmy Carter.

Shortly after he moved into the White House, President Carter asserted that the status of both the Panama Canal and the Canal Zone had to be changed. "I believed that a new treaty was necessary," the president wrote in his memoirs. "I was convinced that we needed to correct an injustice."[4]

Besides his belief that the United States was morally obligated to return to Panama land within its borders, President Carter had another compelling reason to initiate a new arrangement with Panama. General Torrijos had made menacing threats that Panama could no longer peacefully accept the subservient conditions that the 1903 treaty had imposed on his country. Military advisers warned President Carter that if fighting broke out between Panama and the United States, at least 100,000 American troops would be needed to protect the canal. Even with such a large force, if warfare began, it would be impossible to guarantee that the canal would not be the victim of sabotage committed by angry Panamanians.

TWO NEW TREATIES

Teams of diplomats began negotiating a new relationship between Panama and the United States. After months of arguments, concessions, and compromises, they produced two important treaties in August 1977. The treaties were signed by General Torrijos and President Carter on September 7 in a Washington, D.C., ceremony attended by representatives from most Latin American nations.

The first treaty dealt with operation of the canal and sovereignty over the Canal Zone. The second treaty involved the defense of the canal.

In the first treaty the United States accepted a stunning reversal of its longtime policies regarding the canal. The United States agreed to give up its possession and control of the canal on December 31, 1999. At that time Panama would become the sole owner and operator of the waterway.

During the period before the end of 1999, a new U.S.

government agency called the Panama Canal Commission would manage, operate, and maintain the waterway under the direction of a nine-member board. The commission would be composed of five Americans and four Panamanians. Its chief officer would be an American until 1990; after that date the head of the commission would be a Panamanian. In addition to its other responsibilities, the commission was directed to hire a larger number of Panamanians for canal-related jobs.

The annual U.S. fee paid to Panama for use of the canal was increased to $10 million. From canal tolls, Panama was to receive an additional $10 million yearly. Even more important, Panama was to be given 30 cents for each ton of shipping that moved across the waterway. (In the 1980s the total yearly revenue that Panama gained from the canal amounted to as much as $80 million.)

The question of sovereignty over the Canal Zone was resolved entirely in Panama's favor. American sovereignty there was to end as soon as the treaty went into effect. After that date the Canal Zone would no longer exist; Panama would govern that area as part of its own territory.

This far-reaching treaty was welcomed enthusiastically by the Panamanian people. Rómulo Bethancourt, Panama's chief treaty negotiator, said joyfully, "Getting control of the Canal Zone and the canal is one of Panama's oldest national desires. To generation after generation of Panamanians, the canal has symbolized the country's national patrimony [inheritance]—in the hands of foreigners. We developed a kind of national religion over the canal."[5]

The second treaty, called the neutrality treaty, concerned the defense of the Panama Canal in the future. Although the United States would continue to have prime responsibility for the protection of the canal, it would now share that responsibility with Panama.

SIGNING IS ONLY HALF THE BATTLE

Even though both treaties had been signed by Torrijos and Carter, the battle for their acceptance had just begun. Still to come in Panama was a national plebiscite (vote of the people) to decide whether the citizens approved the treaties. In the United States the Senate would have to ratify the treaties, and then both houses of Congress would need to pass bills that implemented (carried out) various provisions of the agreements. Sol Linowitz, a member of the U.S. team that had forged the treaties, wrote, "We all recognized that we had done only the first half of the job. What we did not understand yet was that the first half had been less arduous, less complicated, and less emotional than the task that lay ahead."[6]

When the plebiscite was held in Panama, the citizens voted overwhelmingly to accept the treaties. In the United States Congress, however, the fate of the treaties was much less certain. "I knew that we were sure to face a terrible fight in Congress," President Carter later said.[7]

Carter was told that only thirty-seven senators could be counted on to support the treaties, while twenty-five senators definitely opposed them. Since ratification of all treaties by the Senate requires a two-thirds vote, at least thirty of the thirty-eight undecided senators had to vote for ratification, or the Panama treaties would be rejected.

Democratic senators generally favored the treaties, and many Republican senators declared they would vote against them. But the battle over ratification was not a strictly partisan issue. Some Democrats in the Senate deserted the Democrat in the White House and opposed the treaties. On the other hand, former Republican President Gerald Ford supported ratification, and so did some Republican senators.

Republican Howard Baker Jr., the Senate minority leader, strongly endorsed the agreements with Panama.

President Carter worked hard to convince the undecided senators that the Panama treaties would benefit the United States by removing the growing threat that some form of military action might be taken against the canal. He also insisted that under the new arrangement American vessels, including warships, would continue to have access to the canal. Gradually Carter won over many of the doubtful senators.

Just when it seemed that the long campaign on behalf of the treaties was nearing victory, Senator Dennis DeConcini, an Arizona Democrat, proposed an amendment to the neutrality treaty that became a roadblock on the path to ratification. His amendment stated: "If the Canal is closed, or its operations are interfered with, the United States of America shall have the right to take such steps as it deems necessary to reopen the Canal or restore the operations of the Canal, as the case may be."[8]

The serious problem posed by this amendment was that it would change one treaty and thereby force the government of Panama to hold another plebiscite, this time on the revised treaty. General Torrijos and the Panamanian press strongly denounced the DeConcini amendment and called it another attempt by the United States to dominate its weaker neighbor. Torrijos angrily declared that he could not promise that the people of Panama would again vote to approve the so-called neutrality treaty, especially if it included an amendment that improved the position of the United States at their expense.

At first Senator DeConcini refused to withdraw his amendment, but later he accepted a compromise. He would not add his amendment to the treaty itself—thus avoiding the necessity of a second plebiscite—but he would include it instead as a "reservation" in the Senate resolution that introduced the subject of ratification.

RATIFIED AT LAST

Many weeks of heated debate passed before the Senate ratified the treaties in March and April of 1978. Both treaties were approved by a vote of sixty-eight to thirty-two. This was only one vote more than the two-thirds minimum. The only other treaty ratification struggle that compared in length and intensity with the Panama debate was the one in 1919 and 1920 over whether the United States should join the League of Nations—which the Senate rejected.

It is impossible to know whether General Torrijos would have taken military action if the Senate had turned down the Panama treaties. After ratification he claimed that if the treaties had failed in the Senate, the next day he would have given orders to the National Guard to blow up the canal.

The implementation of the canal treaties now moved to the House of Representatives. Laws were needed to deal with such subjects as the operation of the Panama Canal Commission created by the new arrangement, the relocation of civilian canal workers and military forces, and the transfer of U.S. property to Panamanians. One bill that was passed by both houses of Congress put the Panama Canal Commission under the control of the Department of Defense and required it to seek yearly approval from Congress for its funds and activities.

Members of the House of Representatives, having to run for reelection every two years and knowing that a large number of Americans opposed the so-called Panama giveaway, acted cautiously and slowly to provide the measures needed to carry out the provisions of the treaties. Following lengthy debate, the House finally voted by the narrow margins of 200–198 and 204–202 to pass the bills implementing the treaties. Then the Senate approved the House bills.

Sixteen months had passed between the Senate's ratification of the first Panamanian treaty and the time when Congress adopted the implementation measures in September 1979. Not until three days before the treaties took effect and the United States ended its sovereignty over the Canal Zone (October 1, 1979) was President Carter able to sign the implementing legislation.

The Panama treaties had an important effect on the careers of some politicians in both the United States and Panama. Six senators who had voted for the treaties failed to be reelected in 1978 as did another eleven in 1980. Senator Howard Baker's attempt to win the Republican presidential nomination in 1980 was unsuccessful, partly because of his strong stand in support of the unpopular treaties. One of several reasons why President Carter was defeated in his bid for reelection in 1980 was the vigorous role he had played in achieving a new relationship with Panama.

In Panama Omar Torrijos considered the treaties the crowning accomplishment of his nearly ten years of serving as his country's powerful ruler. He announced in October 1978 that the time had come for Panama to become a more democratic nation. Torrijos gave up his day-to-day management of the government and resumed his command of the National Guard. The new chief of state was his handpicked president, Aristides Royo, who was named to this position by the National Assembly.

On July 30, 1981, Torrijos was killed in an airplane crash. His death set the stage for the most ominous chapter in Panama's history.

*Manuel Noriega in 1987 at the height of
his power as "maximum leader" of Panama*

6

~ ~ ~

A RUTHLESS DICTATOR: MANUEL NORIEGA

Manuel Antonio Noriega was born in 1934 in a Panama slum, the illegitimate son of an accountant and a maid. His father gave Manuel the Noriega name but paid little attention to the child and his mother. Some sources say that Manuel's mother died when he was five years old; other sources say she abandoned her son.

The young boy then went to live in a single-room tenement apartment with a schoolteacher whom he called Mama Luisa. She encouraged him to overcome poverty by getting a good education. Manuel earned high grades at the National Institute, considered the best public high school in Panama City.

Manuel grew up in a rough neighborhood, where fistfights, barroom brawls, shootings, and prostitution were common. He was small for his age and tended to be the victim of attacks by larger boys. Biographer John Dinges wrote, "His survival depended on outthinking and outtalking those who threatened him. But he was caught and beaten enough that by the time he was a teenager he often carried a small pistol."[1]

After Noriega graduated with honors from high school, he wanted to become a doctor or psychologist. Too poor to pay tuition, he tried to win a scholarship to the University of Panama Medical School. His failure to win one of these coveted scholarships was a permanent source of resentment. Many years later—after he became his country's dictator—Noriega would taunt the upper-class Panamanians by saying that their greatest mistake was hoarding all the medical school openings for themselves.

Noriega scraped together enough money to take courses in medical laboratory technology and hoped for a chance to transfer into medical school. He was working at a hospital taking blood samples when he happened to meet a high-school classmate, Boris Martínez. Noriega bitterly complained that he was not earning enough money to pay for any more university classes. Martínez talked enthusiastically about his own career choice; he was about to graduate from a military school and expected to qualify for a commission as a second lieutenant in the Panamanian National Guard.

A MILITARY CAREER

After thinking about what Martínez told him, Noriega decided that a military career offered the opportunity for him to escape a life of poverty and obscurity. He got in touch with his half brother, Luis Carlos Noriega, who was serving in a minor post in the Panamanian embassy in Lima, Peru.

Luis arranged a scholarship for Manuel to study at Peru's Chorrillos Military Academy.

Some of the academy students made fun of Noriega's appearance. His heritage included blacks, Indians, and whites, and his skin was darker than that of many Peruvian classmates. Manuel had a stocky physique with a bull neck, and he stood only five feet five inches tall. His face was badly pockmarked from acne, and teasing students called him *cara de piña*, or "pineapple face." (Even after he became the most powerful man in Panama, his enemies referred to him—behind his back—by this derogatory nickname.)

Apparently Noriega was a cadet at the military academy when he was first recruited by U.S. agents to report on the political beliefs of his fellow cadets. These young men were potential leaders in their Latin American countries, and the U.S. Defense Intelligence Agency (DIA) wanted to know which ones might have communist leanings. Noriega was paid $20 a week for spying on his classmates, and the DIA continued to pay him for information even after he was arrested for beating a prostitute.

On his return to Panama in 1962, Noriega was commissioned a second lieutenant in the National Guard and was stationed at Colón, where he became a close associate of Omar Torrijos. By 1968 Noriega had been promoted to the rank of first lieutenant and had become a paid informant for the U.S. Central Intelligence Agency (CIA). In October of that year he joined Torrijos and the other military leaders who overthrew President Arias. Stationed in the province of Chiriquí, Noriega swiftly seized the radio station and telephone lines in the city of David, effectively cutting off all communications with Panama City.

We have already seen how in 1969 Noriega played a significant role in quashing the unsuccessful coup against Torrijos and returning the general to power. Torrijos richly rewarded him for his support with a promotion to lieutenant colonel and made him chief of military intelligence, known as the G-2 unit.

Noriega thrived in his position as Panama's number-one spy. He kept complete files on all Panamanian political and military leaders, including information on their personal lives that could be used for blackmail. While continuing his CIA ties, Noriega extended his contacts to other countries, including Communist Fidel Castro's Cuba.

He was available to carry out secret missions for the United States—for a price. At the request of the Nixon administration in 1971, he quietly went to Havana to obtain the release of the American crews of two Florida-based freighters that Cuba had refused to turn over to American authorities. On the other hand, sometimes Noriega worked against the interests of the United States. For example, he bought eavesdropping tapes from several Canal Zone U.S. sergeants he had recruited, and he may have passed the stolen information to Castro.

NORIEGA GROWS MORE POWERFUL

The administration of President Richard Nixon had declared a war on drugs, and it was embarrassed to learn in 1972 that Noriega was heavily involved in drug trafficking. He was using Panama as the transshipment base for smuggling narcotics from Colombia, the chief drug-producing country, into the United States. Noriega was making millions of dollars from this illicit trade. At the same time he was being paid by U.S. authorities for giving them valuable information about other drug traffickers in Panama.

Officers in the U.S. Bureau of Narcotics and Dangerous

Drugs considered possible ways to end Noriega's drug trafficking. One option was to have him assassinated, but the officers quickly agreed it "wasn't such a good idea, that it would be inappropriate and unnecessary."[2] No effective action to halt Noriega's drug trafficking was agreed upon, and the CIA kept him on its payroll.

As Noriega grew more powerful, he became more daring and ruthless. In 1975 his G-2 agents kidnapped various businesspeople and broadcast executives who were critical of the Torrijos government. Their possessions were seized, and these prominent citizens were exiled to Ecuador. On another occasion the G-2 agents broke up a women's group that was opposing the government's oppressive treatment of women. Among those arrested was the daughter of a former leader of the National Assembly. She was held in a filthy jail while false charges that she was a thief were concocted.

Noriega served as the head of intelligence operations, enforcer of drastic punishment, and chief troubleshooter for General Torrijos, who once introduced him as "my gangster." By the late 1970s Noriega was the most feared and perhaps the most hated man in Panama. "I know that I have an image problem," he told Sally Quinn in an interview for the *Washington Post* (March 8, 1978). "Mine is a position that doesn't attract sympathy. But somebody must do this job. . . . In Panama there is only one force that has control. That's my job."[3]

After the death of Torrijos in 1981, President Royo lost the support of the National Guard and was forced to resign. In 1983 the guard's top officer also stepped down, providing the opportunity for Noriega to become commander of the guard. Later that year he combined the National Guard with the smaller navy and air force to form the Panama Defense Forces (PDF). Noriega promoted himself to the rank of general and had control of about fifteen thousand PDF members.

In the 1984 presidential election the candidates were Arnulfo Arias, the eighty-three-year-old former president, and economist Nicolás Ardito Barletta, a cabinet officer during the Torrijos era and a former vice president of the World Bank. At that time Panama was saddled with a huge national debt. Both Noriega and U.S. government officials favored Barletta's election, hoping that he could help Panama's sluggish economy. When it appeared that Arias had won the election, Noriega's henchmen seized the ballot boxes and changed the vote count to put Barletta in office.

President Barletta was only a figurehead; Noriega ruled the country and was willing to sell his services to anyone who would pay the price. On behalf of high officials in the administration of Ronald Reagan, Noriega secretly sent weapons to the Contras to use in their rebellion against the Sandinista government in Nicaragua. This was at a time when the United States Congress had banned further aid to the Contras, but President Reagan was determined to continue helping the Contras, whom he described as "freedom fighters." Noriega's undercover role in aiding the Contras was the chief reason why the United States continued to pay him and was slow in condemning his other criminal actions.

Noriega developed another lucrative, illegal business— money laundering. Huge drug profits from the cocaine cartel in Colombia were flown into Panama and deposited in international banks. Then the money was recycled ("laundered") by being transferred into the state bank of Panama, where it escaped detection by bank authorities. Banks processed billions of dollars this way, and Noriega pocketed large commissions by serving as the middleman in these unsavory transactions.

Among Noriega's other rackets was selling fake passports and visas to Cubans and Libyans who wanted to enter the United States. He also shipped high-tech equipment to Cuba, which was then sent to the Soviet Union, in defiance of a U.S. ban on such trade. And he became a double agent in dealing with the rebellion in nearby El Salvador. He sponsored flights of arms supplies to the guerrilla forces and at the same time sold information about the rebels' strategy to the Salvadoran government and the CIA.

EXPOSING THE CRIMES

Dr. Hugo Spadafora was one Panamanian who had the courage to speak out against Noriega's crimes. In March 1984 he boldly told a reporter for Panama's largest newspaper that "it is truly shameful that today . . . the uniform of every single member of the National Guard is stained by the activities which Noriega has been carrying on for years now, activities such as drug trafficking, weapons contraband, and political manipulation."[4]

Spadafora continued to openly lash out against the criminal pursuits of Panama's dictator. This infuriated Noriega, who decided that his enemy's voice must be silenced. When Spadafora was returning by bus from a trip to Costa Rica, G-2 agents seized him shortly after the bus entered Panama. They tortured him mercilessly and then, while their victim was still alive, beheaded him. His body was dumped inside the Costa Rican border in a U.S. mailbag.

The discovery of Spadafora's headless, mutilated body shocked the Panamanian people, who demanded that the murderers be brought to justice. President Barletta announced that he was forming an independent commission to investigate the horrible crime. This prompted Noriega to remove Barletta from office and replace him with Vice President Eric Delvalle as the puppet head of state. United States government officials strongly protested Barletta's forced resignation, but Noriega paid no attention to their complaint.

In June 1986 investigative reporter Seymour Hersh wrote articles for the *New York Times* in which he revealed that Noriega was a CIA agent of long standing who was involved in murdering, election fixing, drug trafficking, and money laundering. Hersh asserted that what he was saying was already known in the White House.

Public opinion in both Panama and the United States was now sharply turning against the ruthless dictator. Congress, the State Department, and the Justice Department all clamored for his removal. But the CIA and the Department of Defense wanted to keep him in power to continue aiding the Contras and protecting the Panama Canal.

Noriega, however, felt he could weather the storm because of his important services to the CIA. "The U.S. is like a monkey on a chain," he declared. "All you do is play the music, and the monkey performs."[5] He assumed that the crisis in his relations with the United States would pass if he kept playing Contra music. And he asserted that "false" stories about his activities were leaked to hard-line conservatives in the United States who were looking for an excuse to scuttle the 1978 treaty that would return the Panama Canal to his country in the year 2000.

In June 1987 Roberto Díaz Herrera, Noriega's chief of staff, tried to persuade his boss to resign as head of the Panama Defense Forces. Noriega's angry response was to demand that Díaz Herrera retire from his high position as second-in-command of the PDF. This enraged Díaz Herrera, who as a loyal insider had knowledge of the dictator's many criminal activities. He publicly announced that Noriega had accepted millions of dollars in return for permitting drugs to pass through Panama and large payments for laundering money and securing Panamanian passports and visas for Cubans. He also claimed that Noriega had rigged the 1984 election to put Barletta in the presidency, ordered the murder of Spadafora, and even had a hand in plotting the airplane crash that killed Torrijos (which has never been proven).

"The Díaz Herrera charges were the political equivalent of a 7.0 Richter-scale earthquake."[6] These accusations were so stunning and overwhelming that they set off widespread street demonstrations by Panamanians determined to have Noriega stripped of power. People in cars blared their horns and shouted that the dictator must go. People on the sidewalks pulled out white handkerchiefs and waved them defiantly. "Each wave was greeted with intensified honking and shouting. A new political movement and a simple pattern of communication had been born."[7]

Noriega responded swiftly and aggressively. He banned public demonstrations, declared a state of emergency, suspended the constitution, and shut down newspapers and radio stations. The dictator dispatched his assault squad—known as the Dobermans—to the home of Díaz Herrera, where he and forty-four of his supporters were arrested. Under extreme pressure, Díaz Herrera broke down and falsely said that his charges against Noriega were untrue. Then he was banished into exile in Venezuela.

Meanwhile the National Civil Crusade, a coalition of Catholic Church leaders, businesspeople, and students, launched a successful two-day strike against Noriega's rule. Dressed in white, their symbol of protest, the crusaders went into the streets, where they loudly banged pots and pans until PDF members squelched their spontaneous uprisings.

Dissidents also accused President Delvalle of being a

coward who took all his orders from Noriega. While Delvalle was attending a party at Panama's luxurious Union Club, other guests, who represented the country's prosperous upper class, shouted that he was a weak puppet and forced him to flee when they reached into their glasses and then pelted Delvalle with a barrage of ice cubes.

MOVING AGAINST THE DICTATOR

After Noriega's crimes were made public, people in the United States were shocked and enraged. On June 26, 1987, the U.S. Senate, by an 84-2 vote, passed a resolution demanding that the government of Panama remove Noriega and investigate the charges against him.

Noriega declared that the Senate vote had insulted him. He ordered all government employees, ranging from office workers and G-2 agents to eight cabinet members, to march on the U.S. embassy in Panama City. Chanting "Yankees go home," the crowd flung paint-filled bags at the embassy walls and smashed the windows with rocks. Cars in the embassy parking lot, a nearby consulate building, and the American library also had their windows shattered. The demonstrators inflicted more than $100,000 in damages to American property.

The attack on the American embassy led to deteriorating relations between the United States and Panama. In the next few weeks the Reagan administration suspended economic and military aid to Panama. Even Panama's request for tear gas from U.S. stockpiles was rejected.

The unrest in Panama severely damaged the nation's banking system. Banking profits accounted for nearly 10 percent of Panama's income, but nervous businesspeople began withdrawing billions of dollars from local banks after the United States cut off financial aid to Panama. As a result the small nation faced enormous problems in making payments on its foreign debt of nearly $4 billion.

The pressure on Noriega to resign continued to mount. "His days are numbered," an American policy maker told Don Oberdorfer for an article in the *Washington Post* (July 23, 1987). "But that number could be dozens, hundreds, or even thousands."[8]

The swarthy dictator refused to concede that the United States could drive him from power. Instead he said that the Americans were plotting to regain control of his country. "I am not a peon of the United States," he exclaimed, "and this commander will not compromise national sovereignty."[9]

TIGHTENING THE VISE

Noriega, however, had not reckoned with the United States legal system. On February 4, 1988, the Department of Justice filed indictments (charges) against him in the Florida cities of Miami and Tampa. These indictments accused Noriega of extensive drug trafficking in Panama, racketeering by providing protection to other narcotics traffickers in return for millions of dollars in bribes, and promoting the laundering of drug profits by Panamanian banks.

For the first time Noriega was shaken by an action taken by the United States. He feared spending years in an American prison. The dictator discussed with his closest advisers the possibility of resigning if an arrangement could be made with the U.S. government to drop the indictments against him. However, each time he discussed this subject, he decided against giving up his power.

Diplomats from the United States met privately with President Delvalle and strenuously urged him to dismiss

Noriega. Delvalle finally summoned the courage to announce publicly that the dictator had been deposed. Panamanians then poured into the streets, honking horns and waving flags and white handkerchiefs. But their celebration lasted no more than half an hour. The PDF soldiers rushed into the streets, and the cheers of the people were silenced by blasts of tear gas.

Noriega quickly ousted President Delvalle and replaced him with Manuel Sólis Palma, the minister of education. So many presidents of Panama had now been sacked that someone described them as "Kleenex presidents" because they all were disposable. Even though Delvalle fled into hiding, the United States continued to recognize him as Panama's legitimate president.

On April 8, 1988, President Reagan announced that the United States was imposing strict economic sanctions on Panama. He cut off all of Panama's yearly payments that came from operation of the canal, froze Panamanian funds that were deposited in U.S. banks, prohibited U.S. companies in Panama from paying local taxes, and stopped all shipments of dollars to the beleaguered Central American country.

That same month more than 5,000 Panamanians marched along one of Panama City's main streets, calling for Noriega's resignation. Again the PDF moved in. While dragging the demonstrators to paddy wagons for the trip to jail, the officers beat them with rifle butts and rubber clubs.

Also in the spring of 1988 about twenty officers in the PDF, led by Col. Leonidas Macias, attempted a coup to overthrow Noriega. It failed, but it convinced the dictator that he could not count on the allegiance of either Panama's citizens or all of its military leaders. Sensing that the end of his regime might be approaching, he held secret negotiations with U.S. diplomats. He almost agreed to leave Panama in exchange for canceling the indictments against him, but in the end he stubbornly chose to remain.

As the vise began tightening on Noriega, officers in the U.S. Pentagon grew concerned that he might attempt some desperate act. Perhaps he might try to blow up the canal, or take hostage some of the thousands of American citizens living in Panama City.

Because of one despicable criminal, the most serious crisis in the relations between Panama and the United States was nearing its climax.

The war of words between Panama and
the United States escalated into armed conflict on
December 20, 1989, when the United States invaded Panama.

7

~ ~ ~

THE UNITED STATES INVADES PANAMA

In 1988 Vice President George Bush was elected president of the United States and inaugurated the following January. Panama, according to its constitution, was to hold its next presidential election in May 1989.

Noriega supported one of his rich business partners, Carlos Duque, to be his next puppet president. The opposition chose lawyer Guillermo Endara as its presidential candidate. Since Panama has two vice presidents, Endara's running mates were philosophy professor Ricardo Arias Calderón and businessman Guillermo (Billy) Ford.

The opposition candidates had an important objective: if elected, they would oust Noriega. President Bush strongly supported these candidates, and the United States government contributed $10 million to their campaign. However, U.S. officials knew there was a danger that Noriega's agents might rig the election to make it appear that Duque had won. If that happened, Secretary of States James A. Baker III told President Bush, "you will be faced with pressures to take additional, stronger steps."[1]

On the day before the election a team of twenty-one U.S. officials, headed by former President Jimmy Carter, flew to Panama to serve as election observers. The voter turnout was enormous, probably the largest in Panama's history. There were few skirmishes at the polling places, and at the end of election day Carter told reporters, "So far its OK. It's the counting that's the problem."[2]

To the U.S. observers who talked to many voters as they left the polls, it appeared that Endara had won in a landslide, probably by a margin of about three to one. But the next day Noriega's election bureau announced that Duque was the victor. What it did not announce was that the election was a fraud. Voter registration lists had been destroyed; PDF members and their families had been ordered to vote "early and often." Ballot boxes had been confiscated; vote counting had been tampered with to ensure Duque's "election." Carter declared emphatically, "The government is taking the election by fraud. It's robbing the people of Panama of their legitimate rights. . . . I hope there will be a worldwide outcry of condemnation against a dictator who stole this election from his own people."[3]

Following the election, the opposition candidates were treated brutally by Noriega's thugs. They lunged past Endara's bodyguards, punching the face of the man who had rightfully been chosen president and knocking his glasses to the ground. When he bent down to pick up his glasses, one of his attackers swung a lead pipe directly at Endara's skull. Blood streamed from his head as he sprawled unconscious.

Endara's vice presidential candidates were also assaulted. Arias Calderón was struck several times. Ford bled profusely from a blow to his head, and seconds later a bullet killed his bodyguard. Miraculously, all three opposition candidates survived and were rushed to safe hiding places.

THE UNITED STATES TAKES ACTION

Reacting angrily to the phony election and the cruel treatment of the opposition candidates, President Bush declared that "the days of the dictators are over."[4] He dispatched 2,000 more troops to bolster the 12,000 personnel of the U.S. Southern Command (armed forces) permanently stationed in Panama. The president announced that American dependents not living on military bases in Panama would be evacuated and the embassy staff reduced by two-thirds. He also decided to invoke a provision of the canal treaty that permitted U.S. troops unlimited training exercises throughout Panama. This was a ploy of psychological warfare designed to give the PDF the message that if it did not remove Noriega, the U.S. military would.

In May 1989 the United States took its case to the Organization of American States (OAS), hoping to gain the support of Latin American nations in its attempt to oust Noriega and help establish a democratic government in Panama. U.S. government officials realized that this mission probably would not succeed when the OAS delegates refused to unseat the Panamanian representative, who was a member of Noriega's inner circle. Many of the delegates were suspicious that the U.S. campaign against Noriega was simply another example of the powerful Colossus of the North intervening in the domestic affairs of a weaker Latin American country. The OAS did produce a resolution condemning "abuses" by Noriega and calling for him to hold new elections. It also sent fact-finding teams to Panama, but it did not demand that Noriega step down.

Instead of holding the new elections requested by the OAS, on September 1, 1989, Noriega appointed a personal friend, Francisco Rodriguez, to serve as provisional president. The United States then broke off all official diplomatic relations with Panama.

American leaders worried about what might occur on January 1, 1990—the date when, according to the 1978 canal treaty, a Panamanian was scheduled to become head of the Panama Canal Commission. The canal could be in extreme danger if an officer appointed by Noriega held this important position.

On several occasions the CIA, the Southern Command, and other U.S. agencies that still had contacts with the PDF signaled its leaders that the escalating crisis could be resolved if they would stage a successful coup to overthrow Noriega. "In truth," said Secretary of State Baker, "we were doing our best to foment [promote] a coup."[5]

It was widely known that some members of the PDF had grown frustrated with their stubborn dictator and his harsh policies. They also were beginning to suffer financial hardships because the economic sanctions imposed by the United States were taking a heavy toll on Panama's national income. In October the government was unable to pay the wages of PDF members. The time for a coup appeared to be fast approaching.

On the evening of October 1 the wife of PDF Major Moises Giroldi secretly contacted a U.S. intelligence agent stationed at the Southern Command headquarters. Her husband, she said, was organizing a coup against Noriega and needed a little help from the U.S. military. He wanted American troops to block two streets near the Comandancia (the PDF headquarters) so that Noriega could not use these routes to bring in reinforcements once the coup began.

Some U.S. intelligence experts were skeptical about Major

Giroldi's scheme. Giroldi had played a large part in suppressing the 1988 coup led by Col. Leonidas Macias. Was he now a genuine rebel eager to oust Noriega, or was he still a loyalist, planning some incident to embarrass the United States?

On October 3 U.S. authorities realized that the coup was a legitimate effort to unseat Noriega. The rebels stormed the Comandancia and captured Noriega as he was approaching his headquarters. Giroldi could have executed Noriega or turned him over to U.S. authorities. Instead, he pleaded with his boss to resign as commander of the PDF. Foolishly, he allowed his captive more than half an hour to make private phone calls that no one overheard. Giroldi thought these calls might be to Noriega's family; instead, the wily dictator was ordering loyal PDF members to come to his rescue.

U.S. troops had blocked the two streets leading to the Comandancia as they had been asked to do. U.S. helicopters flew over the PDF headquarters, but did not provide any assistance to the rebels. Noriega's loyalist forces bypassed the two closed roads and took another route to the Comandancia. They easily overwhelmed the rebels and freed their dictator. When he was back in control, Noriega swiftly ordered the executions of about three dozen conspirators, including Giroldi.

THE CRISIS ESCALATES

The failure of the coup angered and frustrated U.S. government officials, who wondered why American forces had not collaborated with Giroldi to make his mission successful. Congressman Henry Hyde complained that during the rebellion U.S. military personnel looked "indecisive, vacillating, and weak."[6] President Bush was very unhappy that a serious window of opportunity had been lost.

Now feeling confident that there would never be a large-scale U.S. attack in Panama, Noriega lashed out in increasingly hostile statements about U.S. aggression directed against him and his country. On December 15 he ordered the National Assembly to pass a resolution declaring Panama "to be in a state of war while the aggression lasts." The resolution further stated, "To confront this aggression, the job of chief of government of Panama is hereby created, and Manuel Antonio Noriega is designated to carry out these responsibilities as maximum leader for national liberation."[7]

The night after the National Assembly declared a state of war against the United States, two incidents occurred that elevated the war of words into a military conflict. An unarmed U.S. marines officer was shot to death by a Panamanian soldier as he tried to drive through a PDF roadblock. That same evening a navy lieutenant and his wife were stopped by PDF guards. The navy reported that the lieutenant was repeatedly kicked in the groin and that his wife was sexually harassed.

These incidents prompted President Bush to finally take military action against Noriega. "He's gone too far," the president told his advisers. "Enough is enough."[8] Later Bush told the American public that there were four reasons why the United States invaded Panama: to protect American lives, to bring Manuel Noriega to justice, to enforce the Panama Canal treaties, and to restore democracy in Panama.

Shortly before the war began, U.S. authorities brought together the three opposition candidates of the May elections—Endara, Arias Calderón, and Ford. So that Panama would have the semblance of a new democratic government, a secret ceremony was hastily arranged to swear into office President Endara and his two vice presidents.

In the early morning hours of December 20, 1989, nearly 10,000 soldiers, sailors, marines, and air force personnel joined the 14,000 Americans already stationed in Panama. The name of their mission was Operation Just Cause.

Not since World War II had an airborne operation of this magnitude been attempted. As many as 285 U.S. aircraft took part in the campaign. AC-130 Spectre planes attacked the Comandancia and surrounding areas, firing bullets, rockets, and 105 mm artillery. Another 110 helicopter gunships landed hundreds of troops in dozens of positions. Together with tanks and armored vehicles, American troops seized the PDF headquarters and prevented Noriega loyalist units in the countryside from entering Panama City. Most of the heavy fighting was completed within the first day, and the Americans achieved a total victory over their Panamanian foes.

Exploding shells and tracer bullets started huge fires in the El Chorrillo tenement district near the Comandancia. Wooden structures burst into flames and collapsed, and when desperate residents ran into the streets many fell under the torrent of firepower from the skies. The flames razed nearly 2,000 dwellings, leaving about 15,000 people homeless.

After the PDF soldiers were overwhelmed, sniping continued for several days. Some of the snipers were members of Noriega's battalions who changed to civilian clothes and shot at Americans and at fellow Panamanians supporting the U.S. cause. A more serious problem was that as soon as the PDF collapsed, there was no existing police force in Panama's cities and towns. A rash of widespread looting then occurred. Many stores and shops were broken into by vandals, who carried off wide assortments of wares, ranging from food and liquor to expensive jewelry and TV sets. Some thieves resold the stolen products at cut-rate prices. Merchants had to call on their relatives and friends to bring any weapons they could find—guns, knives, or clubs—and help stand guard around-the-clock at the entrances to their stores.

Twenty-three American servicemen lost their lives in Operation Just Cause. Three American civilians—including one woman schoolteacher—were also killed. Neither the U.S. authorities nor the government of Panama could provide an accurate total of the Panamanian casualties, partly because many victims were buried in mass graves. Southern Command first announced that it believed that 314 PDF soldiers had been killed but later revised the figure downward to 50. Estimates of the civilian death toll ranged all the way from 202 to 4,000.

A TEMPORARY ESCAPE

The American mission in Panama had been successful, except for one important factor—General Noriega had not been captured. He had gone into hiding when the invasion began, and even though U.S. intelligence agents explored every lead, they were unable to find him. As the days passed and the embarrassment mounted, the hunt was intensified.

Finally on Christmas Eve, after five days of searching, the fugitive was spotted in a restaurant parking lot in Panama City. By the time American soldiers arrived on the scene, Noriega had vanished. A few moments later it was learned that he had taken refuge in the Vatican embassy. By long tradition, embassies provide sanctuary (a safe place of refuge) for persons seeking protection, usually for political reasons, so U.S. troops could not enter the Vatican embassy in Panama City and seize the elusive general.

Armored vehicles flanked the embassy gates, and crowds of angry Panamanians gathered in front of the building, shouting for their hated dictator to surrender. Even a psychological device was used: day and night loudspeakers blared rock music at such a deafening level that it was hoped Noriega would come outside because he could no longer stand the ear-piercing roar. But Monsignor José Sebastián Laboa, who was in charge of the embassy, told the trapped dictator he would not force him to leave.

For the next nine days U.S. diplomats appealed to Laboa and also to the Catholic Church officials at the Vatican in Rome to expel Noriega. They stressed that the fugitive in the embassy should be considered a drug-dealing criminal rather than a politician entitled to sanctuary. As Americans began fearing that Noriega might stay in the embassy for years, Laboa tried valiantly to convince him to surrender voluntarily.

Finally on January 3, 1990, Noriega left the embassy and was taken into custody by U.S. servicemen. He gave no reason for his change of heart, but apparently he feared that either U.S. forces would eventually storm the embassy or that he would be captured, perhaps tortured, and murdered by his own countrymen. He was whisked by helicopter to an airport and then flown to Florida to stand trial.

Most Panamanians were overjoyed and relieved to be rid of their despised "maximum leader." They fervently hoped that military dictatorship would be replaced by democracy and civilian rule in their country. Leaders of most Latin American nations also applauded the end of Noriega's ruthless regime, but some criticized the United States for again using military might to force its will on a weaker country south of its borders. And experts in international law questioned the legality of one nation kidnapping and prosecuting the chief of state of another nation.

Author Frederick Kempe claimed that the use of massive military force against Panama "was the final proof of the failure of American foreign policy in Panama." The invasion, he contended, "was an indictment of the United States' thirty-year affair with General Noriega, a relationship that had begun with his furtive recruitment into espionage as a young military cadet and ended with Noriega as Federal Prisoner 41586."[9]

A ship approaches a lock on its way through the Panama Canal.

8

~ ~ ~

PANAMA AND THE UNITED STATES TODAY

Manuel Noriega has not been treated like an ordinary inmate at the Metropolitan Correctional Center near Miami, where he has been held in custody since 1990. He was granted the status of a prisoner of war, which permitted him to wear his PDF uniform in court appearances and to receive visits from Red Cross officials, who periodically check to see that he is not being mistreated. As a prisoner of war he also is paid $59 a month by the U.S. government.

The former dictator is housed in a suite consisting of a bedroom/cell, private shower, office, and conference room. His office contains several chairs, a desk, two computers, a copier, and a shredder. In his quarters he has a color television and an exercise bicycle. He plays tennis and basketball with his guards, who also bring him meals and library books.

A phone is kept nearby on a guard's desk. Whenever Noriega wants to use it, he gives the guard the name and phone number of the person he is calling. Often he calls relatives and friends in Panama. Prison authorities can listen to and tape all of his conversations, except those between him and his attorneys.

NORIEGA IS CONVICTED

In 1992 jurors in a federal district court convicted Noriega of criminal charges that included drug trafficking, money laundering, and racketeering. The judge blocked testimony about Noriega's alleged role in providing arms shipments to the Contras in Nicaragua, and he rejected as irrelevant the presentation of secret records from a 1983 meeting between Noriega and Vice President George Bush. "There's more than meets the eye in the Noriega case," said Dick Gregorie, one of the attorneys who developed the evidence against Panama's former leader. "But nobody wanted to push certain buttons."[1] Since the charges against the defendant did not include helping the United States supply arms to the Contras at a time when Congress had decreed that such aid was illegal, the public remained uninformed regarding the extent of Noriega's activities on behalf of the Contras.

Noriega was sentenced to a forty-year term in prison. After the trial prosecutors attempted to have him moved from his plush quarters in Florida to a maximum-security prison in Marion, Illinois, but this request was denied by the U.S. Federal Bureau of Prisons.

In 1993 a court in Panama convicted Noriega of ordering the 1985 torture and slaying of Hugo Spadafora, the outspoken political opponent who had dared to reveal the criminal pursuits of his country's ruler. Although Noriega did not appear at the trial in Panama, he was sentenced to twenty years in prison. Because he already was a prisoner in the United States, the verdict in Panama had no effect except to express the Panamanian people's extreme displeasure at the criminal actions of their former "maximum leader."

The Noriega case in the United States surfaced again in 1995 when his lawyers filed a motion for a new trial. They cited new evidence that the U.S. government had made a secret deal with the Cali drug lords in Colombia in order to convict Noriega. (The Cali cartel, or business syndicate, controls about 80 percent of the world's cocaine market.)

The new evidence indicated that the U.S. government had persuaded the Cali cartel to compel a key witness, Ricardo Bilonick, to surrender to U.S. authorities and testify against Noriega. In exchange, the defense lawyers claimed, U.S. government officials offered to reduce the prison sentence of Luis Santacruz Escheverri, a high cartel leader, from twenty-three years to fourteen years. As the co-owner of a cargo airline that had shipped twenty tons of cocaine into Miami in the 1980s, Bilonick testified in court that he was thoroughly familiar with the way that Noriega had used Panama as a base for receiving drugs from Colombia and then shipping them to the United States.

Noriega's lawyers charged that the Cali cartel gave Bilonick a $1.2 million bribe to testify against Noriega. They claimed that by not revealing at the trial that witness Bilonick had been bribed, prosecutors had infringed on their client's constitutional rights.

Bilonick denied taking a bribe and said that he testified against Noriega because the U.S. government had agreed to give him only a short sentence for his own drug trafficking and to allow him to keep more than $1 million in drug profits. Transcripts of the trial showed that the judge had called

Bilonick one of the government's "most important witnesses."[2] Prosecutors, however, argued that Bilonick was not a "star witness" and was only one of more than forty persons who took the stand to testify against the dictator.

In March 1996 a federal judge refused to order a new trial for Noriega. His lawyers have the right to appeal this decision to a higher court.

AIDING PANAMA

Shortly after the American invasion of Panama, President Bush proposed that the United States give that country $1 billion in economic aid. Congress appropriated $420 million for this aid—less than half the amount Bush had requested.

Some of the money was used for emergency relief, including housing for 3,000 families displaced by fires and other damages brought about by Operation Just Cause. Loans were made to many small businesses looted during the invasion, and credit was extended to companies that had suffered losses as a result of the warfare.

The Panamanian economy rebounded sharply in 1990 and 1991; it grew at a rate faster than that of most other countries. With Noriega out of power, businesspeople, especially in Japan and the United States, believed that Panama was now a safe place in which to invest their money. The optimistic economic reports, however, masked a serious problem: in 1990 between 30 and 35 percent of the Panamanian people were unemployed, and an estimated 44 percent of the population lived in poverty. These figures were slightly reduced later in the 1990s, but unemployment and poverty still are major concerns in Panama.

Crime was another serious problem that had to be dealt with. President Guillermo Endara replaced Noriega's military-based PDF with the civilian-controlled Public Force (PF). The United States helped train members of the PF to perform policing and other security duties. Some of the people who joined the new force had been members of the PDF, and this raised the question of whether it could remain free of military control. Many Panamanians feared that the PF might not be strong enough to guarantee public safety, and this led to the creation of more than one hundred private security forces, employing about 10,000 people.

Normal operations of the Panama Canal resumed immediately after Operation Just Cause. The 1978 Panama–United States treaty had provided that in 1990 a Panamanian would replace the American who headed the Panama Canal Commission. This change occurred as planned, and Fernando Manfredo became the canal's chief administrator.

Although the development of other routes has reduced the importance of the canal in United States trade, 13.4 percent of U.S. shipborne commerce flowed through this waterway in 1994. Annually, 4 percent of world trade passes through the Panama Canal, and in 1994 vessels from seventy-eight countries used the canal. Japan, Chile, Ecuador, and Peru, in addition to the United States, are its chief users.

THE ONGOING DRUG PROBLEM

An alarming sign of trouble to the Endara government was the growing realization that Panama's role in drug trafficking had not ended with Noriega's ouster. Drug dealers in Colombia continued to find Panamanian land, air, and sea routes attractive avenues for their smuggling activities. Panama's government was unable to adequately patrol its extensive coastlines. (The combined length of Panama's Caribbean and Pacific coastlines is nearly equal in length to the east coast of the United States.) The country lacked sufficient radar coverage and did not have enough trained agents to cope with the many drug dealers.

Panama's rugged, almost inaccessible jungles also were very difficult to patrol. In a September 1990 report the U.S. State Department's International Narcotics Bureau stated that it suspected a laboratory for refining cocaine was operating in Darién province, which borders Colombia. "Its existence," declared one Latin American expert, "is at minimum a glaring sign of the government's inability to police its own territory."[3]

Despite its handicaps, the Panamanian government stepped up its campaign against narcotics traffickers. In 1991 authorities seized nearly ten tons of cocaine, double the amount taken the previous year and almost twice what was seized in the entire ten years before Noriega's downfall. Panama signed agreements with the United States calling for complete cooperation between the two nations, including joint patrols, in the war against drugs.

Still the problem persisted. At the end of 1992 Ariel Alvarado, Panama's secretary for drug affairs, reported that during that year 6.2 tons of cocaine were seized at or near Colón, which since the U.S. invasion had become the main port of entry for the illicit drug trade. "Five shiploads of drugs enter Panama every day," Alvarado said.[4]

DIFFICULTIES WITH ENDARA

In the first weeks of President Endara's administration, opinion polls indicated that the new leader was very popular with the Panamanian people. But within a few months his approval rating slipped from about 90 percent into the teens. One of the problems was that Endara and Panama's two vice presidents often disagreed about policies. These three men, who had been brought together in a hastily formed coalition when the invasion began, represented three separate political parties, and they had different opinions about how the government should be run.

The Endara government was accused of helping the relatively few wealthy people and doing little to improve the lives of the many poor people. "This government has taken so much and given it all to so few," said Marco Gandasegui, one of Panama's leading historians. It "actually rewrote the tax code to raise taxes on the poor and cut taxes on those with incomes over $100,000."[5]

The Endara administration kept in office many of the government workers who had served during the Noriega regime, including members of the PDF. Retaining these workers made it difficult for other Panamanians to find government jobs. It also permitted the supporters of Noriega to conduct guerrilla warfare from within against the new civilian government, and they "were thus able to use their positions to try to destabilize the new government."[6]

Confidence in the Endara administration lagged as a wave of murders and robberies made city streets in Panama much more dangerous than they had been before the invasion. People wondered whether the police were on their side or on the side of Noriega's henchmen, who were commonly blamed for the rising crime wave.

Fear reached a new height in March 1990 when a grenade was tossed from a car into a crowded Panama City bar, killing a U.S. serviceman and wounding twenty-seven other people. The terrorist shouted "Viva Noriega!" before he drove away. He was never captured, but the Twentieth of December Movement (M-20), which opposed the United States invasion, claimed responsibility for the vicious act.

Later, members of M-20 conducted a series of attacks directed against U.S. servicemen and installations, and they may have been responsible for setting off explosive devices outside the homes of two members of Endara's cabinet.

A CBS–*New York Times* opinion poll taken in 1990 showed that 92 percent of the Panamanian people approved President Bush's launching of Operation Just Cause. So in 1992 when the American president stopped at Panama City en route to a conference in Brazil, he anticipated a warm welcome from Panama's citizens. After meeting with President Endara, Bush was driven to a big park where about 15,000 people had gathered to hear him speak.

Before Bush could address the crowd, a group of about 150 anti-American protesters began throwing rocks and bottles at police who had cordoned off the area. The police immediately fired tear gas to disperse the demonstrators. Clouds of gas drifted across the park, causing many among the audience to panic and flee. The American president and his party were moved quickly into armored limousines and whisked away from the area by security guards and U.S. Secret Service agents.

A few hours later President Bush gave his speech at an air base outside Panama City. Referring to the incident that had occurred that afternoon, he told Panamanians that "no little left-wing demonstration is going to set your democracy back."[7]

NEW ADMINISTRATION, RENEWED COOPERATION

A presidential election was held in Panama in May 1994. Since that country's president is limited to a single five-year term, Endara was not eligible to seek reelection. More than 70 percent of the adult citizens voted. Unlike many of Panama's previous presidential contests, the 1994 election was not tainted by any signs of fraud. Former President Jimmy Carter, who observed the polling places and the vote counting, reported that every aspect of the election was honest.

Businessman Ernesto Perez Balladares won a narrow victory, gaining 33 percent of the votes in a field of seven candidates. He edged out Mireya Moscoso de Gruber, the widow of three-term president Arnulfo Arias. She received 29 percent of the votes. Finishing third with 17 percent of the votes was Ruben Blades, a popular salsa singer and actor. Under Panamanian law a majority vote (one more than half) is not required to win a presidential election, so Perez Balladares was declared the winner, even though he had only about one-third of the votes. He was inaugurated on September 1, 1994.

President Bill Clinton met with President-elect Perez Balladares at the White House in July 1994. Both leaders expressed their commitment to a close and cooperative relationship between the United States and Panama. They said that this spirit would guide their efforts to ensure a smooth transfer of the Panama Canal and American-occupied properties to full Panamanian control by or before December 31, 1999. President Clinton reaffirmed that the United States would honor all its commitments expressed in the two 1978 treaties.

The American president welcomed Perez Balladares's pledge to stem narcotics-related money laundering in Panama and offered U.S. technical assistance to help Panama achieve that goal. At the same meeting Perez Balladares told Clinton that he intended to promote his country's economy by increasing Panama's trade with other countries in the Western Hemisphere.

Panama was one of the countries that joined the new Association of Caribbean States (ACS), which was founded in July 1994. Comprised of twenty-five nations with borders on the Caribbean Sea, the ACS aimed to establish a free-trade group within the next ten years. Once the ACS is in operation the countries in this group would no longer place tariffs on products traded among themselves. The Association of Caribbean States then would become the fourth-largest trading block in the world, serving a combined 200 million people. The first summit meeting of the ACS nations was held on the island of Trinidad in August 1995.

One of the problems that plagued the United States in the summer and fall of 1994 was the large number of Cubans fleeing Communist Cuba for U.S. shores. About 30,000 refugees crowded onto rafts and small boats for the 100-mile trip from Cuba to Florida. President Clinton asked Panama to accept some of these refugees, who were overflowing the holding camps in the United States.

The Panamanian government agreed to house as many as 10,000 Cubans at U.S. bases in Panama for a period of up to six months. The United States assumed all expenses involved in the operation and promised that American military personnel would police the refugees.

Some of the nearly 9,000 Cubans at the holding camps in Panama rioted against U.S. soldiers in December 1994. Apparently they were protesting their prolonged detention and the uncertainty about their future. The rioting injured more than 200 U.S. soldiers and 28 Cubans. It was not ended until 500 additional troops were airlifted to Panama from Fort Hood in Texas and Fort Bragg in North Carolina.

A QUESTION OF U.S. PRESENCE

Panama has not been free of domestic troubles in recent years. In January 1995 ten members of the police force were arrested on charges of plotting a coup that was to have included the assassination of President Perez Balladares. Later that year four people were killed, dozens were injured, and five hundred were arrested in a pro-union demonstration on the first day of a general strike called by forty-nine union organizations. The demonstration turned violent when riot police attempted to break down barriers set up by protesters to block off some of Panama City's major streets. Lasting eight days, the strike brought a temporary halt to a large part of the country's economy.

In 1995 the United States turned over two bases, Fort Davis and Fort Espinar, to Panama, as provided for in one of the 1978 treaties. Before the end of 1999 the United States is planning to return to Panama property comprising about 77,000 acres and 4,272 buildings, as well as full control of the Panama Canal. The U.S. Southern Command, which currently has about 8,000 military personnel, is scheduled to move to Florida in 1998.

As the time for the evacuation of United States interests in Panama approaches, many Panamanians are not in favor of a complete U.S. withdrawal. They fear both its economic and political impact. In a 1995 poll 71 percent of Panama's population believed that their country's economy would suffer from a total U.S. pullout because Panamanians would lose about 16,000 military-related jobs and about $460 million that Americans spend yearly in Panama.

In the same poll 75 percent of the Panamanians said that they wanted to retain the United States military presence beyond the year 2000. This was a striking reversal of opinion from earlier years, when most of the nation's people clamored for the removal of all U.S. troops from their soil. Many Panamanians had changed their minds about the value of U.S. military forces in their country after they witnessed more than two decades of political instability, government corruption, frequent coup attempts, political assassinations, bloody strikes and demonstrations, and the failure of the local police force to cope with the crime issue. As Fernando Manfredo, the administrator of the Panama Canal, said, "Panamanians lack confidence in their government, so that makes them want the U.S. to stay."[8]

In March 1995 Anne Patterson, U.S. deputy assistant secretary for inter-American affairs, addressed this subject when testifying before a subcommittee of the House of Representatives. She said that the 1978 neutrality treaty with Panama "includes specific language confirming that the treaty would not prevent the two countries from making arrangements or agreements . . . for the stationing of [U.S.] military forces or the maintenance of defense sites to fulfill their responsibility of maintaining the canal's neutrality after 1999."[9]

President Clinton and President Perez Balladares met on September 5, 1995, and opened discussions about the possibility of a continued U.S. military presence in the area of the Panama Canal after the scheduled departure of U.S. troops. No final decisions were reached at this meeting.

This is an extremely delicate subject—one that has to be handled with great care and deliberate caution. The presidents of both countries are determined not to reignite the violent riots and demonstrations that preceded the Carter–Torrijos treaties. Ways must be found to guarantee Panama that it will be a completely sovereign nation, with or without United States military personnel on its soil.

As the twenty-first century nears, the relations between Panama and the United States are entering a new stage that seems to hold the promise of cooperative endeavors, greater harmony, and mutual respect.

PANAMA AND THE UNITED STATES: A CHRONOLOGY

1917	Panama enters World War I against Germany
1933	President Franklin D. Roosevelt proclaims Good Neighbor policy
1941–1945	United States defends Panama in World War II
1959	Riots erupt over flying Panamanian flag in Canal Zone
1961	United States launches Alliance for Progress and Peace Corps
1964	Balboa High School flag incident causes 24 deaths
1968	Omar Torrijos assumes power in Panama
1977	Carter-Torrijos treaties are signed
1978	Carter-Torrijos treaties are ratified
1979	United States ends its sovereignty over the Canal Zone
1981	Torrijos is killed in plane crash
1983–1989	Dictatorship of Manuel Antonio Noriega
1987	Unsuccessful attempt to depose Noriega
1988	U.S. Justice Department files charges against Noriega
1988	United States imposes economic sanctions on Panama
1989	Failed coup to overthrow Noriega
1989	U.S. forces invade Panama
1990	Noriega is seized and sent to Florida to face trial
1990	Civilian President Guillermo Endara replaces Noriega

1992	Noriega is convicted in Florida court
1994	Ernesto Perez Balladares is elected president
1994	Panama joins Association of Caribbean States
1999	United States is scheduled to transfer the canal and American-held properties to Panama

SOURCE NOTES

Chapter 1

1. Peter Winn, *Americas: The Changing Face of Latin America and the Caribbean* (Berkeley: University of California Press, 1992), 449.

2. Ana María B. Vázquez, *Panama* (Danbury, Conn.: Childrens Press, 1991), 73.

3. Edward F. Dolan, *Panama and the United States: Their Canal, Their Stormy Years* (Danbury, Conn.: Franklin Watts, 1990), 20.

Chapter 2

1. Edmund Lindop, with Ernest W. Tiegs and Fay Adams, *Latin America* (Lexington, Mass.: Ginn, 1983), 27.

2. William J. Jorden, *Panama Odyssey* (Austin: University of Texas Press, 1984), 23.

3. Dolan, *Panama and the United States*, 37.

4. Judith St. George, *The Panama Canal: Gateway to the World* (New York: Putnam, 1989), 19.

5. Clifford Krauss, *Inside Central America: Its People, Politics, and History* (New York: Summit Books, 1991), 251.

6. St. George, *Panama Canal*, 22–23.

7. Eric Zencey, *Panama* (New York: Farrar, Straus, Giroux, 1995), 374.

Chapter 3

1. David G. McCullough, *The Path Between the Seas: The Creation of the Panama Canal, 1870–1914* (New York: Simon and Schuster, 1977), 249.

2. Walter LaFeber, *The American Age: United States Foreign Policy at Home and Abroad Since 1750* (New York: Norton, 1989), 226–227.

3. McCullough, *The Path Between the Seas*, 323.

4. Krauss, *Inside Central America*, 253.

5. McCullough, *The Path Between the Seas*, 373.

6. Krauss, *Inside Central America*, 254.

7. LaFeber, *The American Age*, 230.

8. Miles P. Du Val, *Cadiz to Cathay: The Story of the Long Struggle for a Waterway Across the American Isthmus*, 2d ed. (Stanford: Stanford University Press, 1947), 438.

9. Thomas A. Bailey and David M. Kennedy, *The American Pageant: A History of the Republic*, 7th ed. (Lexington, Mass.: D.C. Heath, 1983), 590.

10. St. George, *Panama Canal*, 57.

11. Ibid., 68.

Chapter 4

1. Michael L. Conniff, *Panama and the United States: The Forced Alliance* (Athens: University of Georgia Press, 1992), 80.

2. Paul B. Ryan, *The Panama Canal Controversy: U.S.*

Diplomacy and Defense Interests (Stanford: Hoover Institution Press, 1977), 24.

3. J. Lloyd Mecham, *A Survey of United States–Latin America Relations* (Boston: Houghton Mifflin, 1965), 314.

4. Ibid., 115.

5. Ryan, *The Panama Canal Controversy,* 36.

6. Jorden, *Panama Odyssey,* 30.

7. Conniff, *Panama and the United States,* 115.

8. Jorden, *Panama Odyssey,* 64.

9. *New York Times,* March 22, 1964, 1.

Chapter 5

1. Conniff, *Panama and the United States,* 130.

2. Michael Barone, *Our Country: The Shaping of America from Roosevelt to Reagan* (New York: Free Press, 1990), 570.

3. Gary Wills, *Reagan's America: Innocents at Home* (Garden City, N.Y.: Doubleday, 1987), 330.

4. Jimmy Carter, *Keeping Faith: Memoirs of a President* (New York: Bantam, 1982), 570.

5. Krauss, *Inside Central America,* 261.

6. Sol Linowitz, *The Making of a Public Man* (Boston: Little-Brown, 1985), 77.

7. Carter, *Keeping Faith,* 155.

8. Jorden, *Panama Odyssey,* 520.

Chapter 6

1. John Dinges, *Our Man in Panama: How General Noriega Used the United States and Made Millions in Drugs and Arms* (New York: Random House, 1990), 32–33.

2. Ibid., 63.

3. Quoted in *Current Biography,* March 8, 1988, 429.

4. Frederick Kempe, *Divorcing the Dictator: America's Bungled Affair with Noriega* (New York: Putnam, 1990), 130.

5. Kevin Buckley, *Panama: The Whole Story* (New York: Simon and Schuster, 1991), 59.

6. Guillermo de St. Malo A. and Godfrey Harris, *The Panamanian Problem: How the Reagan and Bush Administrations Dealt with the Noriega Regime* (Los Angeles: The Americas Group, 1993), 26.

7. Ibid., 27.

8. Quoted in *Current Biography*, March 8, 1988, 428.

9. Buckley, *Panama*, 115.

Chapter 7

1. James A. Baker III, *The Politics of Diplomacy: Revolution, War and Peace, 1989–1992* (New York: Putnam, 1995), 182.

2. Buckley, *Panama*, 178.

3. Ibid., 179.

4. Baker, *The Politics of Diplomacy*, 183.

5. Ibid., 185.

6. Ibid., 187.

7. Buckley, *Panama*, 225.

8. David S. Behar and Godfrey Harris, *Invasion: The American Destruction of the Noriega Regime in Panama* (Los Angeles: The Americas Group, 1990), 9.

9. Kempe, *Divorcing the Dictator*, 418.

Chapter 8

1. Cathy Booth, "Noriega Makes His Case," *Time*, February 17, 1992, 33.

2. "Star Witness?" *Newsweek*, December 4, 1995, 6.

3. Linda Robinson, *Intervention or Neglect: The United States and Central America Beyond the 1980s* (New York: Council on Foreign Relations Press, 1991), 132.

4. Barbara Jamison, "Promises Broken, Illusions Lost," *The Nation*, March 15, 1993, 336.

5. Marc Cooper, "In Panama, No People's Choice," *The Nation,* May 9, 1994, 631.

6. Steve C. Ropp, "Panama: The United States Invasion and Its Aftermath," *Current History,* March 1991, 115.

7. *Facts-on-File,* June 18, 1992, 443.

8. Linda Robinson, "Some Mixed Signals for Uncle Sam," *U.S. News and World Report,* October 25, 1993, 37.

9. *U.S. Department of State Dispatch,* March 20, 1995, 229.

FURTHER READING

Barry, Tom, and Deb Preusch. *The Central American Fact-book*. New York: Grove Press, 1986.

Behar, David S., and Godfrey Harris. *Invasion: The American Destruction of the Noriega Regime in Panama*. Los Angeles: The Americas Group, 1990.

Dolan, Edward F. *Panama and the United States: Their Canal, Their Stormy Years*. Danbury, Conn.: Franklin Watts, 1990.

Griffiths, John. *Take a Trip to Panama*. Danbury, Conn.: Franklin Watts, 1989.

Lindop, Edmund, with Ernest W. Tiegs and Fay Adams. *Latin America*. Lexington, Mass.: Ginn, 1983.

Markun, Patricia Maloney. *Central America and Panama*. Danbury, Conn.: Franklin Watts, 1983.

———. *The First Book of the Panama Canal*. Danbury, Conn.: Franklin Watts, 1958.

McCullough, David. *The Path Between the Seas: The Cre-*

ation of the Panama Canal, 1870–1914. New York: Simon and Schuster, 1977.

Nicolay, Helen. *The Bridge of Water: The Story of Panama and the Canal.* New York: Appleton-Century, 1940.

Rink, Paul. *The Land Divided, the World United: The Story of the Panama Canal.* New York: Julian Messner, 1963.

St. George, Judith. *The Panama Canal: Gateway to the World.* New York: Putnam, 1989.

Vázquez, Ana María B. *Panama.* Danbury, Conn.: Childrens Press, 1991.

INDEX

ABOUT THE AUTHOR

Edmund Lindop graduated summa cum laude from the University of Southern California and earned his master's degree in history at the same university.

Panama and the United States is Edmund Lindop's thirty-seventh book for young people. Since the mid-1990s, he has written six other books for Twenty-First Century Books: *Political Parties* in the Inside Government series and five books in the Presidents Who Dared series.

Among his other recent books are *The Changing Supreme Court, Assassinations That Shook America,* and *Presidents by Accident.* Lindop's books about Latin American subjects include *Cuba: A First Book* and a textbook in a social studies series.

For thirty-eight years Lindop taught history and government classes at the middle-school and high-school levels in Los Angeles, where he lives with his wife, Esther. He trained new social studies teachers at three universities.